PSYCHIC SUFFERING

PSYCHIC SUFFERING

From Pain to Growth

Gemma Corradi Fiumara

LONDON AND NEW YORK

First published 2015 by Karnac Books Ltd.

Published 2018 by Routledge
2 Park Square, Milton Park, Abingdon, Oxon OX14 4RN
711 Third Avenue, New York, NY 10017, USA

Routledge is an imprint of the Taylor & Francis Group, an informa business

Copyright © 2015 to Gemma Corradi Fiumara.

The right of Gemma Corradi Fiumara to be identified as the author of this work has been asserted in accordance with §§ 77 and 78 of the Copyright Design and Patents Act 1988.

All rights reserved. No part of this book may be reprinted or reproduced or utilised in any form or by any electronic, mechanical, or other means, now known or hereafter invented, including photocopying and recording, or in any information storage or retrieval system, without permission in writing from the publishers.

Notice:
Product or corporate names may be trademarks or registered trademarks, and are used only for identification and explanation without intent to infringe.

British Library Cataloguing in Publication Data

A C.I.P. for this book is available from the British Library

ISBN 9781782202691 (pbk)

Edited, designed and produced by The Studio Publishing Services Ltd
www.publishingservicesuk.co.uk
e-mail: studio@publishingservicesuk.co.uk

CONTENTS

ABOUT THE AUTHOR	ix
INTRODUCTION	xi
Creating a conceptual space	xi
The question of limitations	xv
A communal enterprise	xxi
"Not necessarily an illness"	xxiii
The abhorrence of suffering	xxvi
CHAPTER ONE	
Creative and uncreative suffering	1
Winnicott's legacy	1
The alternative route that is also an alternating one	3
The question of agency and passivity	7
CHAPTER TWO	
Psychic anaesthetics	15
Sara and her drugs: resisting anaesthesia	15
From temporary to permanent	20
Familiarity with inner pain	26
The role of ideologies	30

CHAPTER THREE
Psychic "justice"	39
A concern for psychic "justice"	39
Fate as the default of destiny	45
From the "social" to the "psychological"	53

CHAPTER FOUR
The shadow revisited	61
Percival and the engineering sanctuary	61
Confronting the shadow	66
The default of projective strategies	69
Dr Jekyll: a case that is not so strange	74

CHAPTER FIVE
The relational outlook	77
Winnicott and Hegel on personal confrontations	77
Empathic allies and the fixity of roles	84
Company *and* solitude	89
The wish to gain and loss aversion	93

CHAPTER SIX
The question of endurance	99
Nirmala: patiently resisting non-existence	99
The less travelled path	104
Travelling the path	110

CHAPTER SEVEN
The challenge of interpretation	117
The use of metaphor	117
The problem of literality	122
The question of psychic effort	126
The experience of relief	131

CHAPTER EIGHT
Moving forward	137
The idea of forward moving	137
Negotiating (with) painful emotions	143
The "teens" transition	148

CHAPTER NINE
Psychic growth 153
    Pain and psychic growth 153
    Construction and deconstruction 156
    Repetition compulsion revisited 159

REFERENCES 163

INDEX 169

*To my little granddaughters
Olivia and Camilla*

ABOUT THE AUTHOR

Gemma Corradi Fiumara has a BA at Barnard College of Columbia University, where she studied as a Fulbright exchange scholar, as well as a doctorate at the University of Rome where she has been teaching ever since. A former Professor of Philosophy at the Third University of Rome, she is also a training analyst with the Italian Psychoanalytic Society. Her books include: *Philosophy and Coexistence*; *The Other Side of Language: A Philosophy of Listening*; *The Symbolic Function: Psychoanalysis and the Philosophy of Language*; *The Metaphoric Process: Connections Between Language and Life*; *The Mind's Affective Life: A Psychoanalytic and Philosophical Inquiry*; *Spontaneity: A Psychoanalytic Inquiry*; and *Psychoanalysis and Creativity in Everyday Life: Ordinary Genius*.

Introduction

Creating a conceptual space

From a generally humanistic perspective, questions primarily exist if there is a cognitive/cultural space for them to develop. We cannot simply ask the question, what is psychic suffering? This concern is a worthy focus of attention only if we are, or become, interested in the everyday modes of our inner pain, which may be evident or inconspicuous. Although our most disparate forms of psychic distress cannot be approached as factual research, once we have captured the intensity of the question, we can further develop our qualities of observation and clinical interaction. This epistemic space is the prerequisite for new perspectives.

This book endeavours to show ways in which to talk and think about the enormous problem of a "gravitational force" surrounding us: an excessive fear of pain that might ultimately paralyse our maturation, growth, and creativity. Is there anything that we could do to cope with this pervasive mental restriction? The very least that we can do is defend an epistemic and affective space in which to recognise and articulate our confrontation with inner pain. The more the problem is shared, the more we can count on relational empathy for this confrontation. As an illustration, if we generally agree that hunger on our planet is unjust, we may then count on the legitimacy of the issue whenever we try to raise it.

Since the effort to perceive and metabolise inner pain is a very demanding enterprise, there seems to be a constant antagonistic pressure to either ignore it completely or else fiercely fight to escape it. Philosophers lend us little perspective: they have a partiality for clear streams, and tend to avoid the paradoxes of our human swamps (Haybron, 2010, p. vii). Inner pain is a paradigm of complexity, and, in trying to approach the issue, you might find yourself talking about some of the most difficult and shadowy phenomena. Not even poets seem up to the task. Difficult and shadowy, yes, but also germinal and promising. Maybe we have just to become involved, and herein lies our choice: between using inner pain or being overwhelmed by it— and we cannot use what overwhelms us. These reflections might even seem to counsel silence, ignorance, or mute rebellion. But why be silent? The celebrated remark of Wittgenstein comes to mind, "Whereof one cannot speak, thereof one must be silent" (Wittgenstein, 1981, p. 89). This might sound censorious and quite at odds with the logic of psychoanalysis. The enormous maturational impetus that is gained by any tentative articulation can never be undervalued. A suffering, confused individual might respond to Wittgenstein's statement by saying, "If that of which I am incapable of speaking is what invalidates my relational life, why should it be precisely that which cannot be said?" This work, therefore, attempts to offer another perspective on affective distress and to explore ways to engage with it clinically, theoretically, and socially. Perhaps, by following this path, we will also uncover its creative value for all.

What characterises the basic attitude of psychoanalytic interpretations is the constant effort to render psychic life more acceptable, more fluid, more expressible, and approachable/bearable enough for us to move forward. It is a painstaking effort to deliver the analysand from the commonly experienced escapes into pathology, somatisation, and stupor. Interpretations not only lead us to discover different and tolerable ways to confront pain, but *also* to experience it rather than simply escape it. However acute, inner pain often tends to resist symbolisation. We need a fellow sufferer to explore, reveal, and name it in such a way that the mute, ineffable distress may reach a higher level of legitimacy. The very fact that some evanescent, but constraining, feelings can somehow be expressed renders us more capable of negotiating with them. If they can be shared, at least by one person, they seem to begin to claim legitimacy *and* admission into the "alchemy" of our inner life. Conversely, when painful emotions cannot be verbalised, they remain inaudible, unknown, virtually non-existent on a conscious level, but even more coercive on an unconscious one (Corradi Fiumara, 1990). From a psychoanalytic perspective, in fact, we ultimately aim to replace an uncreative sort of suffering with a creative, enhancing kind. It is as if, in a world dominated by the food industry, we were paradoxically advocating the beneficial effects of fasting. The challenge in our topic lies in increasing the intelligibility of matters that often seem hopelessly inscrutable. To some extent, this can be done. In analysis, we gain not only a microscopic view of inner phenomena, but also a backstage view of our vicissitudes, virtually devoid of social embellishments. We hope to utilise these "visual" instruments in pursuit of our concern. Also, our wonderful psychoanalytic notions are "true" as far as they go; what we have to be concerned about is whether they go far enough. Nevertheless, I would like to state that my work is primarily conducted from a psychoanalytic perspective that is essentially focused on pathological psychic pain. It is not addressed, therefore, to an exploration of our common, human, existential suffering.

Since we are at the stage of "simple" introductory remarks, let me introduce, as an example, just a few significant quotes without any attempt to establish a coherent, sequential connection between them. We read in Freud, for instance, 'In discussing the subject of mourning . . . I found that there was one feature about it which remained quite unexplained. This was its peculiar *painfulness*". He continues, "Thus the problem becomes more complicated: when does separation from an object produce anxiety, when does it produce mourning and when does it produce, it may be, *only* pain?" (Freud, 1926, p. 169; my emphasis). *Only* pain? This is an insightful remark. This discussion adumbrates the more widespread question of the open, persistent problem of coping forever with psychic pain, with *our* human suffering. In another context, Freud considers a situation which we believe we understand, the situation of an infant who is in danger of losing a person: "That it does have anxiety there can be no doubt; but the expression of its face and its reaction of crying indicate that it is *a feeling of pain*" (Freud, 1926d, p. 170; my emphasis).

Klein synthetically expresses the problem in these terms:

> We recall the fact that the motives and purpose of repression are simply the avoidance of "pain" . . . If a repression does not succeed in preventing feelings of "pain" (or anxiety) from arising, we may say that it has failed. (Klein, 1964, p. 89)

Then again, it is difficult to assess how we actually "repress" our inchoate contact with reality—inner or outer. Moreover, repression contributes to our ignorance. Bion, perhaps, provides an appropriate answer to this point, especially where he says, "There are patients whose contact with reality presents most difficulty when that reality is their own mental state". The difficulty is the fear of discovering the *"feeling* of dread, or anxiety, or mental pain". He elaborates, "*What* it is that they will not suffer or discover we have to conjecture from what we learn from patients who *do* allow themselves to suffer" (Bion, 1970, p. 9). Indeed this is a seminal source. These patients are our mentors, therapists, our ordinary geniuses. In another instance, Bion states,

> Recently I had the occasion to draw the attention of one or two people with analytic experience . . . to the fact that they are beginning to believe that there really is such thing as mental *hurt*. It is difficult to believe because verbal communications are carried out . . . so that words like "anxiety", "embarrassment" and so on have very little meaning. Nobody really believes that they mean anything, but in the consulting-room *"embarrassment" means mental pain.* (Bion, 2005, p. 63)

Nothing less than that—and *very clearly* stated.

If there is an uncreative inclination to anaesthetise all inner pain by whatever means (somatisation, evacuation of the mind, self-deadening, for instance), we cannot approach the problem with the *same* mental outlook, that is, the same logic, which is subjacent to the problem itself. However, what could be a different approach to this unfortunate, widespread attitude? The chapters of this book are all different attempts to answer this question with the help, of course, of those who have already tried to do so. These chapters share the underlying theme of the creative use of human suffering, and each tackles the theme from a different angle.

If we simply acquiesce to limiting views of inner pain, they might exhibit perverse synergies when taken together. In an accompaniment to this enterprise, I shall present three stories involving suffering, three possible stories among many. These are not meant as classic clinical cases, but as attempts at psychobiography introduced for the purpose of illustrating perspectival views of mental suffering. These struggling subjects could illuminate our attempts to effect a reconnection with one's "shadow" (Percival, Chapter Four), to surmount dependence on psychotropic drugs (Sara, Chapter Two), and to enable re-emergence from ineffable pain (Nirmala). Perhaps they are emblematic stories of psychic vicissitudes reflecting the general thesis: the creative use of suffering.

The question of limitations

What we might call *happiness* might not be the primary end of psychoanalysis—and not even of life, after all. In fact, our celebrated recent aspiration to happiness-for-all perhaps only amounts to the better or worse responses to the conditions that obtain, whatever they are. Life gives what it has and not what it does not have; it concedes the happiness that there is in it, and certainly not the happiness that exceeds it. In Lewis's words, "If we will not learn to eat the only food that the universe grows, the only food that any possible universe can ever grow, then we must starve eternally" (Lewis, 2012, p. 47). We need help constantly to see inner life anew and to be aware of rationalistic, melioristic outlooks: ultimately, theories that somehow purport to surmount our human limitations. We try here to engage with different, challenging concerns that may enhance a fuller recognition of our limits. Perhaps we should craft new strategies for dealing with the most relevant of our psychic problems: coping with our inner limits and finitude. It is through this approach that we aim to expand on the theme of psychic pain. In a transition of perspectives, we try to move from an outlook dominated by "Hegelian", triumphal ways of thinking towards a complementary domain of coexistence with pain and adversity. This is, of course, a paradoxical coexistence, but it is a creative process which ultimately supports the legitimisation of our limitations. A great deal of work remains to be done in this respect. In the present work, I draw not only from our psychoanalytic culture but also, occasionally, from our philosophical traditions, integrating them into a more complex exploratory process.

In the outlook that I propose, we can better uncover the beneficial aspects of our unavoidable suffering. These creative aspects are generally overlooked in a culture that abhors and devalues frustration and also idealises every occasion for gratification, irrespective of its long-term value (Davies, 2012, p. 113). Liberal optimism perhaps rests on a questionable view of human nature. In fact, we might not be well equipped for the pursuit of happiness, perhaps even tending unwittingly to be the pursuers of *un*happiness. This might be the case even when we possess the freedom to fashion our lives according to our own designs (Haybron, 2010, p. 227). An outlook of liberal optimism may even reverberate in the presentation of the so-called clinical material, invariably with some kind of a happy ending, together with confirmation of our underlying theses. There is often serious, cumulative trauma in the clinical cases presented, just as in the cases I introduce in the present work. It is as if we were saying, "Just look, and be impressed"—secretly celebrating the wonders of psychoanalysis. By means of our amazing psychoanalytic methods and the efforts of a dedicated analyst, major developments can be demonstrated. This seems to be a classical paradigm in the presentation of clinical cases.

Paradoxically, as analysts, we continue indefinitely through inner vicissitudes of conviction and uncertainty that are somehow congruent with our work. We must continuously learn to doubt more radically than would be admitted in other professions, but also we must often acknowledge a need to believe more fully than is deemed acceptable in our critical culture (Downing, 2000, p. 4).

In *To Have Or To Be?*, Fromm reminds us that "The achievement of wealth and comfort for all was supposed to result in unrestricted happiness for all" (Fromm, 1995, p. 2). Yet, the contribution derived from external circumstances proves quite limited. However, this is not the point of our present concern. What is alarming is the common deduction that if we can only change society, all will be well. This sort of thinking can result in an attitude of stultification. Why? Inevitably, we will look for the source of unhappiness primarily in external conditions. Just change external situations and all will be resolved, we think, and until conditions change we might simply place our own selves in a deadened position—on stand-by, as it were. Let us, for the sake of argument, roughly assume that psychic pain is the opposite of happiness, that experiencing sorrow is the opposite of being happy.

Let us also ask what are the pre-conditions for happiness or pain. In Fromm's well-known classic work, the thesis is that *having* does not ensure happiness, that it is ultimately disappointing, and that only *being* is conducive to whatever happiness we can find in this world. This is a generally acclaimed thesis. What concerns us here is the *provenance* of this "having" mode. The answer to the question, "What is the origin of the having culture?" can be rather disquieting. Of course, *being* is the creative, healthy way of life. But again, where does the *having* come from? There is a risky, common tendency to believe that the unhealthy having mode (engendering disappointment and pain) derives from society, especially from a capitalist, liberal, consumerist society. Of course, this can be the case, although we would be uncritical and benumbed to believe that the unhealthy having mode derives *only* from our unhealthy society—which ultimately amounts to a paranoia. From this we might deduce that if we change society, most of our human distress will be resolved, which is a stultifying attitude. Why? Because we would look for the source of our suffering, or unhappiness, primarily in external conditions, and certainly not in whatever form of inner organisation or idolatry we might harbour.

It is also essential at this point to emphasise the distinction between two different psychological strands. On the one hand, we have an unquestionable desire to improve our living conditions and opportunities. On the other hand, we have a projective, infantilising, paranoid desire to place all danger, wickedness, and adversity outside of ourselves. Conversely, to utilise the appreciation of inner sources of unhappiness in order to blindly disregard issues of social justice would be totally perverse. In my view, an understanding of the centrality of inner actions has nothing to do with our necessary endeavours for social justice, solidarity, equality of rights, and emancipation for each one of us. It would be futile and self-defeating to use one truth to deny another. The overriding belief, however, is that if we just change our external conditions, all will be well in our inner life. A corollary is that until conditions are changed, we might simply put ourselves into a kind of suspended animation, passively waiting for changes to occur.

If we think that the having mode (which impedes the being mode) is induced by a consumerist society, then there is the danger that Fromm's seminal classic *To Have or To Be?* could be interpreted as giving us permission to look for the source of problems primarily, or even exclusively, in our ever-present society. We could, thus, be relieved of the burden of our limitations and from personal effort. There is an insidious problem here: the belief that the having mode derives from sociological factors that conspire for the prevalence of having. Thus, there should be a radical social change that, from the outside, could promote the being mode to which we would happily and judiciously adhere. To this effect, a quote from the back cover of Fromm's book may illustrate this point: "Nothing less than a manifesto of a new social and psychological revolution to save our threatened planet". Fromm is presented as saying that

> Two modes of existence struggle for the spirit of humankind: the having mode, which concentrates on material possessions . . . and is the basis of the universal evils of greed, envy and violence; and the being mode which is based on the pleasure of sharing. (Fromm, 1995, back cover of the book)

Clear enough. But then, a necessary social and psychological revolution seems to be needed, for we have yet to determine the origin of the having mode. Here, we have a very good outlook, but it is not good enough. Why? Because there is an underlying assumption that the pernicious having mode is primarily due to *external* social pressures. Roughly, change the external structure and the problem is solved: the triumph of the being mode is inevitable. This could lead us to a paranoid conviction that the causes of evil are external to us; however, this is simply an expedient, superficial way of avoiding all suffering.

In Davies' comment to Fromm, for instance, we read that "Individuals are compelled by certain social pressures to invest more energy in having and acquiring than developing the art of being" (Davies, 2012, p. 106). This is fair enough, but is this the primary root of our having mode? We would, thus, feel like the victims of maligned social pressures and be inclined to settle for some paranoid outlook whereby the cause of all evils is outside us. If the dominance of the having mode is the outcome of certain consumerist norms which today govern most capitalist economies, we would have to just wait for capitalism to subside for the unhindered triumph of the being mode. We would have simply to hope for, or implement, a radical social transformation. Transformations are, of course, desirable and necessary, but we should also argue that what is needed primarily is a capacity for psychic transformations *and* psychic actions. Perhaps, indeed, not even stable, anti-capitalist structures can usher in the cultural prevalence of the being mode. If we seriously believe that the having affliction is due to a pathogenic social order, then, paradoxically, "revolution" would come to function as the famous "opium of the people". Just suspend your psychic life, wait for change or foster it. The hope of revolutionary solutions might induce a torpor that ultimately impedes silent, psychic creativity. In general, discussions are so frequently focused on the external causes of suffering and pathology, that we may be tempted to ignore the role of inner factors. Both outer and inner determinants can be at work, of course, but inner factors of distress are more often vulnerable to obscurity. This book is also an attempt to create a more balanced approach in the evaluation of determinants. What the reader might retain is the realisation that the stories we tell ourselves about human suffering are limited and limiting stories. There is the expectation here of opening some sort of Pandora's Box, which contains many more possibilities and paradoxes than we would usually take into account.

Hollis seems to suggest that we do not quite have the moral strength to endure the knowledge of our painful conflicts, our struggles with relationships, our multifarious fears, and neither does he assume that we are morally strong enough to act on our insights (Hollis, 2003, p. 7). In Hollis's view, we could even dismiss the issue of psychic pain, for we all have busy lives dealing with outer, pressing, constructive matters that could even permanently solve our inner problems. Almost as if we were exclaiming, "If only society could make life easier for us . . ." Once again, outer reality is blamed for the cause of inner pain; this is yet another expression of the belief in a triumphal, manic solution, accompanied by disregard for the question of limitations and ineliminable paradoxes. Perhaps the belief itself is the source of the problem, but can we develop the capacity to renounce such paranoid outlooks? External causes of pain can often be misleading. In Hollis's view, the covert agenda of unmet needs insidiously burdens relationships, especially those used to anaesthetise our suffering (Hollis, 2003, p. 39). Most relationships fail because we ask too much of them: we want them to relieve us from the burden of living. The narcissistic wounds that are the inevitable result of one's history return in relationships as inappropriate expectations, ineffective strategies, and regressive scenarios. Where personal psychic life is insufficient, we will behave in a needy, controlling, manipulative way. That so many are obsessed with relationships, and keenly disappointed when they do not work, is no wonder, then.

If we perceive that the cause of pain must always be somewhere outside ourselves, we must then constantly expel hurt. According to Lewis, we inflict a great deal more pain on others than we experience ourselves, and we are exploiting this power to the full. Our history is largely a record of strife, war, and terror, with just enough happiness interposed to give us, while it lasts, an agonising apprehension of losing it, and, when it is lost, the poignant misery of remembering (Lewis, 2012, p. 2). Every now and then we improve our collective state of mind a little, and what we call civilisation reappears. In Symington's view, there is a general phobia of affliction, almost as if it were an extinct illness, and that it should be shameful to let it reappear (Symington, 2001, p. 115). This is a quite collective delusion.

Davies judiciously points out that some may contend that if one is not aware of having deep problems, why upset one's contentment by uncovering them? Just live your life and consider it a blessing; still others might claim that a philosophy which says that "being unaware of our deeper problems is itself a problem" (Davies, 2012, p. 69) is a conspiracy against the unproblematic life, that is, a device by which troubled individuals can wreak envious revenge on the more contented. Davies also claims that what these discussions often reveal is the common confusion that many of us experience with respect to the role that problems play in human life. It almost feels as if the absence of problems should be the natural, superior, and preferred state, and the presence of problems the inferior, unfortunate, unnatural state (Davies, 2012, p. 69). This amounts to a very superficial and misleading outlook, for we do, in fact, embody a mind that is constantly processing thoughts. Then again, according to Ferro, "The problem for *homo sapiens* is that he has a mind, a mind which is in need of care if it is to develop harmoniously, and the failures in whose development lead to various modalities of evacuating untransformed beta elements" (Ferro, 2011, p. 57). It is only a short step, in his opinion, to the view that our species has an utterly archaic apparatus for thinking—a mere rough draft of what it could, one hopes, one day become. What, then, could it ideally become? Ferro thinks it could be an apparatus that can afford to be at peace with its more archaic forms, and also capable of managing them. And he continues, "What cannot be alphabetised will be evacuated in hallucinations, psychosomatic illness and unreflected actings-out. This is the source of the 'madness' of the species we see around us" (Ferro, 2011, p. 57). If we had been taught to coexist with our very imperfect condition, and if we had been trained in this practice, perhaps we could live far more intensively, and waste less time. Complain as we might, we must all become accomplished *virtuosi* survivors.

A communal enterprise

The confrontation with psychic pain is probably a shared enterprise, not the accomplishment of isolated acclaimed geniuses. In fact, I am perhaps just writing what the psychoanalytic community "tells" me to write. Dealing with suffering in a creative way is often more effective as a communal venture, even though primarily attempted individually—quite a paradox. Yet, we live by it. This impetus is more like a response to the summons of a cultural environment than so-called creativity. If you think of a psychoanalytic group, or any other group (in which you are immersed and by which you are formed) as attempting the expression of what is going on, you can be transformed into a more functional and co-operative member of the system. The question of suffering is certainly a perspective to be explored and also a lens worth looking through, one that brings aspects of life which are usually blurred into sharp focus

The effort we make to express our inner world can be seen as both intentional *and* constrained, as historically bound *and* enabling broader perspectives. Contrary to positivist, meliorist ideologies, the effort of self-expression is not an overarching (encompassing) venture distinct from the person's everyday psychic actions. Our actions are also social practices and the medium of their own constitution. All of this effort, moreover, derives from an increasing capacity to listen to the community. A confrontation with our suffering thus becomes more and more a communal enterprise. From this perspective, Davies challenges conventional thinking by arguing that if we understand and manage suffering more holistically, it can facilitate individual *and* social transformation in powerful and surprising ways (Davies, 2012, back cover of the book). This holistic outlook is clearly advocated by Winnicott, when he refers to different forms of home life. In "Cure" in *Home Is Where We Start From*, he writes,

> A sign of health in the mind is the ability of one individual to enter imaginatively and accurately into the thoughts and feelings, hopes and fears of another person; also to allow the other person to do the same with us . . . When we are face to face . . . we are reduced to two human beings of equal status. (Winnicott, 1970; quoted in Phillips, 1988, pp. 12–13)

This probably implies two human beings of comparable suffering (Winnicott's work, in fact, refers to emergency homes in the post-war period). This is perhaps the only status we care about in any variety of authentic relations. To ask one another how to define suffering—its meaning, its origins, and how we should respond to it—is a communal psychoanalytic effort. Davies calls our attention to an unfortunate shift towards the negative vision of suffering, because it is how we view our suffering that will influence how we relate to it (Davies, 2012, p. 62)—that is, whether we relate to it creatively or uncreatively. If we privilege the negative vision, the tendency to believe that there is nothing of value to be derived from adversity, a belief will eventually prevail that renders our relationship with pain entirely uncreative and simply reactive.

Instead, we should develop a language for creatively sharing our pervasive human suffering. How do we communicate suffering to one another? We could refer to Kierkegaard for an enlightening and opportune warning. He points out, "That which in its vast abundance is *essentially* inexhaustible is also *essentially* indescribable in its smallest act, simply because . . . it is everywhere wholly present and . . . cannot be described" (Kierkegaard, 1962, p. xxvii). If we want to become conscious of the indescribable, we ultimately need the help of a community of some kind. We cannot just be silent. We could also invoke here Jung's seminal recommendation: "The reason why consciousness exists, and why there is an urge to widen and deepen it, is very simple: without consciousness things go less well" (Jung, 1934, pp. 358–381). However, for this beneficial consciousness we need communal support (not collective, communal) to strive for this creative awareness in the face of pain. The problem with pain is that we immediately respond to it with anaesthetics, therapies, and remedies. Yet, the point is that we certainly do not need (want?) "cure" at the price of restricting, decreasing, or lessening our inner life. While there is much good to be derived from the modification of behaviour and biochemical interventions, the possible diminution of the person (or psyche) which is practised by many modern therapies is a risky compromise, a temporary act of moral condescension in the face of the potential greatness that we all embody.

"Not necessarily an illness"

Here is an inspiring remark by Winnicott: "Neurosis is not necessarily an illness . . . We would think of it as a tribute to the fact that life is difficult" (Winnicott, 1956, quoted in Phillips, 1988, p. 13). Perhaps life is not simply difficult, but so very difficult, much more strenuous than we tend to believe. In *The Future of an Illusion*, Freud says, 'For the individual . . . life is hard to bear just as it is for mankind in general" (1927c, p. 16). Life's essential difficulty has to be confirmed/validated in mutual listening, and ultimately requires a sufficient communal epistemic space. It is not really important that these remarks come from Winnicott or Freud; it is rather that they are so seminal and appropriate to our times. Davies' contribution in *The Importance of Suffering* is an appropriate response to such challenging views. He reminds us that modern psychiatry has been too lightly reclassifying several aspects of ordinary human life (such as sadness, grief, sorrow, anxiety . . .) by implying that they are mental disorders that require medical treatment (Davies, 2012, p. 2). This so-called mistake occurs because the psychiatrists who write the diagnostic statistical manuals primarily pay attention to the external symptoms presented by the subject, or sufferer, almost as if the perception of symptoms could automatically transform a struggling functional person into a patient deserving pity, detached observation, and "scientific" treatment. Psychiatrists are presumably not interested in how the patient could make use of those symptoms, or how they originate. If a person appears sad or anxious, then it is simply assumed that the "patient" is suffering from a disorder that needs to be cured, as if the proper order of our human existence could not possibly include sadness, anxiety, or unhappiness. That a normal person should engage in a laborious and occasionally unbearable response to certain internal and external conditions seems ultimately unacceptable. In the approach of our current diagnostic manuals (Davies, 2012, p. 2), a question such as, "Am I depressed because I am overwhelmed by suffering, or am I suffering because I am depressed?", would probably not be considered. Psychiatrists tend to establish a confluence of ordinary human feelings into legitimate psychological disorders, and probably for good reason.

Davies tries to explore how the growing influence of the diagnostic statistical manuals is one among several factors propagating the misleading belief that much of our everyday anxiety is a damaging disgrace to be urgently removed (Davies, 2012, p. 104). This is a persuasion increasingly ensnaring us into considering all inner pain as an entirely negative (useless) aspect of our lives. The expansion of this contemporary view can be illustrated by statistical data showing that we are progressively managing our affective problems not as potentially creative experiences, but as intolerable conditions that can be remedied with medicine. Davies also judiciously points out that this has nothing to do with the prudence and wisdom of avoiding severe psychic pain in different areas of mental pathology (Davies, 2012, p. 165). Yet, in a pseudo-parental, unduly protective way, our pharmaceutical industry purports to spare us excessive sorrow, tribulation, and grief. The spreading use of psychotropic drugs might be due to the deceptive assumption that altering a patient's biochemistry is usually the best clinical strategy. The risk is that by denying alternatives or accompaniment to medication, we impose an entirely negative view of suffering. The uncritical prescription of psychotropic drugs could serve to deny the emancipatory work that a more creative use of suffering could allow.

Davies' contribution points to (though not quite demonstrates) where our previous thinking might have been too limited. He writes, "The way in which our socio-cultural environment understands, responds and manages our suffering deeply affects its nature and how it will be experienced" (Davies, 2012, p. 165). No occurrence of suffering presents itself as creative *or* uncreative. Rather, suffering *becomes* either creative or uncreative depending upon how we manage and understand it *once it has arrived*. Its nature is significantly shaped by how we respond to it, and, of course, this is true of most human experiences. The problem is that for some reason we do not consider the use of this tough, paradoxical resource. How can pain be a resource? We typically abhor it, and struggle to remove or anaesthetise it. What Davies perhaps tries to argue is that our managerial, unempathic, superficial attitude makes suffering uncreative. He insists that pain, "will become unproductive simply because it is not being responded to in a way that can release its productive meaning and worth. It is the abhorrent, repelling response that induces unproductive suffering" (Davies, 2012, p. 4). Ultimately, this is a very passive response.

The immense fascination and fruitfulness of our psychoanalytic culture probably derives from the fact that it is an effort to deal with inner pain as such, and use it to the best. Other cognate disciplines and cultural offerings primarily attempt instead to anaesthetise it. A psychoanalyst would never consider saying something like, "Just come see me regularly and I will *deliver* you from all of your inner suffering." Davies seeks "new ways of thinking about suffering which will enable us to relate to it less fearfully" (Davies, 2012, p. 62). He claims that it is ultimately misleading to think that our emotional torments can one day definitely disappear. Loss and disappointment are, after all, inevitable human experiences. It should be emphasised, however, that while the eradication of all suffering is a misguided and omnipotent aspiration, it does not imply the conviction that current levels of suffering cannot be decreased. In his exploration of the *The Importance of Suffering*, Davies clearly argues that the current surge in prescriptions is ultimately supporting an exclusively negative vision of human suffering, as if it were a terrifying, alien entity (Davies, 2012, p. 62). In his view, this happened because those prescribing pharmaceutical remedies do not respond to suffering as a necessary signal to transform our quality of life—a "message" that should be heard rather than ignored. Most importantly, the prescribers of drugs do not respond to suffering as the natural accompaniment of a vital impulse to maturation. By chemically anaesthetising suffering, prescribers convey the idea that suffering is none of that, but, rather, "an encumbering experience from which patients must be simply liberated. It is through this response, in other words, that the value of the experience is defined negatively" (Davies, 2012, p. 62). Following Winnicott, we should, therefore, question the conviction that suffering is always a sign of illness. It is not necessarily an illness, but, rather, a "tribute to the fact that life is difficult" (Winnicott, 1956, quoted in Phillips, 1988, p. 13). A tribute is a payment or a contribution that we make to the challenge of life. What defines illness or health might have less to do with the absence of suffering than with our response when it arises. We could perhaps assess health or illness in terms of whether we manage to respond creatively to our tribulations in such a way that they may contribute to self-formation, *or* even self deconstruction, when necessary. Although different kinds of enlightenment actually do remove some unnecessary hardships from human life, in their inclination to cast every form of suffering in purely *negative* terms, they also induce us to neglect the creative forces that we can derive from our human distress.

The abhorrence of suffering

Kahneman reminds us that loss aversion refers to the relative strength of two motives: we are driven more strongly to avoid losses than to achieve gains (Kahneman, 2011, pp. 302–303). A reference point is often the status quo, but it can also be a future goal: not achieving a goal is a loss while exceeding the goal is a gain. Since the two motives are not equally powerful, we might expect the dominance of negativity. Aversion to failure, and fear of not reaching a goal, is much more compelling than the desire for gain. This is ultimately a bleak prospect for the maturation of human beings. The sloganised insistence on "positive thinking" is an outlook that seems promising, but perhaps it fails because ultimately positive thoughts are far weaker than negative ones. Thus, worrying can become a constant attitude, even if it wastes quality time and energy. Even if worrying is useless, we fear that if we stop, negative things are sure to happen (Kahneman, 2011, p. 303). One would think that this awareness might lead us to make every effort to correct negativity dominance in a therapeutic perspective orientated towards maturity, growth, and creativity. The general goal would be to learn to cope with the negative, painful occurrences. When we consider pain itself—the centre of the whole tribulation system—we must be careful to attend to what we personally know and not to what a general culture of suffering phobia makes us believe. The question of human suffering should be a top priority. There is no reason for this ubiquitous and inconspicuous fear of pain; it can be endured, after all, and when it is tolerated it can also be utilised. We can help one another to confront pain and do something with it. This capacity is the indispensable ingredient in any constructive venture. The opposition to pain might ultimately induce some degree of mental blindness, but creative suffering is still suffering, and, thus, there is always a tendency to avoid it. The negative vision of anguish might not only alter our experience of pain but also alter it in damaging ways. This outlook is shaping a culture in which discomfort must always be shunned and definitely anaesthetised by any means. This is a culture that might deprive us of all creative uses of adversity. As is known, how we deal with an experience affects the very nature of the experience itself. Moreover, while we seek the most disparate ways of eliminating discontent, we lapse and flounder in behaviour that actually increases it and also aggravates our phobia of pain. This is an expanding, perverse, inconspicuous, vicious circle.

In Kahneman's view, "Loss aversion is a powerful *conservative* force that only favours minimal changes from the status quo in the lives of both institutions and individuals. This conservativism helps keep us 'stable'—wherever we are" (Kahneman, 2011, p. 305). It is an inert force that holds our inner life together near a reference point, until it becomes paralysing. For the sake of psychic growth, we may have to join forces intrapsychically and intersubjectively against the enormous power that holds our life together near a deadening reference point. The aversion of loss/pain is a conservative power that favours only proformal changes. Thus, a negative vision of suffering increases uncreative suffering, and also implies an increase in our anaesthetising strategies: from the consumption of anaesthetics to the quest for anaesthetising ideologies. Increasing passivity is the price we pay for our opposition to suffering.

In a psychoanalytic context, even therapists can be seriously tempted by an aversion to pain. In fact, according to Grotstein, "The act of analytic containment is more complex than is ordinarily realised" (Grotstein, 2009, p. 94). "More complex" sounds like a timid euphemism for an experience that can be excruciating. In fact, he speaks of a "passion play". He also reminds us that the infantile portion of the analysand's personality (epitomising those who should be forgiven because they do not know what they are doing) uses projective identification to communicate to the analyst. The analyst uses containment: "That is, he *absorbs* the pain, then *becomes* it, one aspect of which is the analyst's agreement to *be* it—that is to "wear" it". Also, "The analysand can *see* that pain has 'travelled' in psychic space from the subjectivity of the analysand to that of the analyst while the analyst is processing or metabolizing it" (Grotstein, 2009, p. 94). This is a very clear description of what goes on in what we designate with the mild and very acceptable term of "containment". It tells us that the analytic disposition is to be placed at the opposite extreme of pain abhorrence. This is the ordinary genius needed for the analytic practice: to be able to survive together with pain aversion and psychoanalytic containment. For the sake of complete clarity, Grotstein quotes Meltzer, affirming, "The truest meaning of transference is the transfer of mental pain from one person to another" (Meltzer, 1992; quoted in Grotstein, 2009, p. 94). Quite so.

Following Bion, Grotstein also argues that this transference, "cannot take place unless the analysand is able to perceive pain in the analyst—that is, experience the movement of the mental pain across the intersubjective gap" (Grotstein, 2009, p. 94). In order to be absolutely clear and unafraid of causing scandal (but what is scandalous, after all?), Grotstein concludes that "This transfer of mental pain (which I call the 'transfer of demons') constitutes for me psychoanalytic exorcism" (Grotstein, 2009, p. 95). In my estimation, the courage to use this vocabulary has nothing to do with mystical or devotional inclinations. Essentially, it constitutes a vertex of observation that ensures a more realistic and deeper appreciation of psychic reality.

CHAPTER ONE

Creative and uncreative suffering

Winnicott's legacy

According to Winnicott, "The link can be made, and usefully made, between creative living and living itself, and the reasons can be studied why it is that creative living can be lost and why the individual's feeling that life is real or meaningful can disappear" (Winnicott, 1971, p. 69). As the burden of life often implicates psychic pain and tribulation, we can perhaps paraphrase, reframe, this seminal remark and claim that it would be useful to establish a link between creative suffering and suffering itself. Moreover, the reasons why it is that creative suffering can be lost or insufficiently developed, and why the feeling that life is meaningful can vanish should be studied. If we take Winnicott seriously, then an assiduous exploration of creative suffering becomes a preliminary necessity. "In a tantalising way", insists Winnicott, "many individuals have experienced just enough of creative living to recognise that for most of the time they have been living uncreatively ... These two alternatives of living creatively or uncreatively can be very sharply contrasted" (Winnicott, 1971, p. 69). Since a good part of our lives is about enduring difficulty and coping with frustration, we will adopt his distinction and focus throughout the work on the question of either suffering creatively or uncreatively.

In Winnicott's view, when psychoanalysis has attempted to address the issue of creativity, it has largely lost sight of its main theme. In fact, "The creative impulse is . . . something that is present when anyone—baby, child, adolescent, adult, old man or woman—looks in a healthy way at anything or does anything deliberately" (Winnicott, 1971, p. 69). It is appropriate to point out here that the sort of creativity to which we refer is not the celebrated creativity of art and science, but the daily creativeness of our efforts aimed at psychic survival, coexistence, and empathy. If we opt for creativity, it usually becomes a principle of action within the self, an attitude that is infused in our daily struggles (Corradi Fiumara, 2013). Let us not forget that life is just not easy, that it can be a burden and is frequently interwoven with misery. I have, thus, borrowed from Winnicott the seminal suggestion of "creative suffering", to be contrasted with *uncreative* suffering.

The point here is that we can find in Winnicott's legacy a very clear and passionate encouragement to continually explore the inventiveness of our everyday efforts. "The creativity that concerns me here", he says, "is a universal. It belongs to being alive . . . The creativity that we are studying belongs to the approach of the individual to reality" (Winnicott, 1971, p. 68), which frequently can be very tough. Being alive is tantamount as struggling to survive, and the approach of the individual to reality tends to converge with his approach to adversity. A passive, uncreative attitude implies that there is nothing that you can do, and, thus, there is no choice but to ingest this, or subscribe to that. This can be a widespread collusion dragging one towards passivity and never towards psychic agency or internal actions (in contrast to reactions). I see no other problem as clinically and culturally more urgent than this concern for psychic suffering. What is even more relevant is the reason why we remain passive after we have detected the deceptive logic, continuing to say: "Suffer? Nonsense! Just eat that apple"—or some other distraction. Through the inimitable language of Kierkegaard, we could ask:

> Which deception is more dangerous? Whose recovery is more doubtful, that of him who does not see or of him who sees and still does not see? Which is more difficult, to awaken one who sleeps or to awaken one who, awake, dreams that he is awake? (Kierkegaard, 1962, p. 23)

Most of us are aware of the ubiquitous, disquieting problem of psychic pain. Perhaps we see it but cannot quite bring ourselves to look into it.

In fact, creativity enters into virtually every aspect of life, and, therefore, there is no reason why it should not enter into our management of distress; hence our focus of attention on creative suffering. Winnicott again:

> One has to allow for the possibility that there cannot be a complete destruction of a human individual's capacity for creative living and that, even in the most extreme, cases . . . there exists a *secret* life that is . . . being creative. (Winnicott, 1971, p. 68)

This secret life to which Winnicott refers is probably the one most vulnerable to obscurity. However minimal or unnoticed, it is the virtue of our finite condition and the source of our fruitful suffering. Of course, our pathology and vulnerability can break us and induce inexplicable sorrow, but that sorrow can also accelerate our yearning for psychic growth and empathy. Winnicott could appear to imply that, given the ubiquitous nature of inner pain, all of our daily crises could be regarded as extreme cases involving a "secret life". What we need most is a capacity for utilising our very own distress, a capacity for suffering in a fruitful way. Given the considerable presence of pain in our lives, I shall adopt his almost sloganised "creative living" in the complementary form of "creative suffering". As Thiele Rolando remarks, the incapacity to suffer creatively makes it virtually impossible for us to confront interpersonal relationships and entertain the prospect of our limitations and ultimate finitude (Thiele Rolando, 1982, p. 97).

The alternative route that is also an alternating one

The outlook we embrace may free us to think differently about the value of emotional misery and to perceive which beliefs may be misleading. My arguments might contribute to overcoming the widespread aversion to psychic pain that unwittingly paralyses us clinically, theoretically, and even socially. What is needed is an increased capacity to use pain creatively. Many of us, for instance, can hardly bear to apply for a candidacy of any kind for fear of being unable to endure the disappointment of defeat: a paralysing attitude indeed. As is known, suffering becomes either creative or simply painful depending on how we manage and understand it once we have encountered it. Its nature and intensity are significantly shaped by how we respond to it. If suffering is regarded as a worthless experience that should be urgently neutralised with anaesthetic devices of any kind, it will inevitably be fruitless. Instead, we should be able to see that it is "the negative response that produces the unproductive experience", in the words of Davies (2012, p. 165). It is necessary for us to recognise some kind of imprisonment in a vicious circle. We need the understanding that suffering is not always futile or damaging, and the appreciation that it is often instrumental to one's emancipation. Once we abandon the psychiatric view that inner suffering is essentially pathologic, damaging, and useless, we can approach suffering in more hospitable terms. As Davies iterates, "Pain is not always something to be anaesthetised, feared or avoided, but is an experience which, if understood and managed correctly, can facilitate the important process of positive, individual and/or social transformation" (Davies, 2012, p. 3).

Raw inner feelings tell us that suffering, however potentially creative, is still plain hurt and that we should strive to maintain a healthy attitude by staying away from it. It should be emphasised at this point that the advocated alternative, maturational route of creative suffering could be instantly abandoned, recanted, or decried as a detrimental, nonsensical outlook. This simply means that the alternative productive path of enduring pain for the sake of growth can suddenly vanish, and we might be cast adrift. We may then become unwittingly ensnared in rigid schizo-paranoid reactions. This also means that although the path of endurance can be steadily travelled, it can also be suddenly abandoned – as if influenced by oscillations or fluctuations. This ultimately tells us that accepting the advocated creative suffering is an alternative that also alternates with uncreative misery. Davies argues that

> Unproductive suffering, on the other hand, is an *essentially* passive state—it is the state of being gripped by feelings or habits that corrode the integrity and quality of our lives, but the roots of which we do nothing to confront and remove . . . Of course neither of these states is constant, since during any instance of productive suffering all sorts of unproductive regressions and hiatuses can occur. (Davies, 2012, p. 7)

This is especially the case if we have absorbed the widespread negative vision that all suffering is something to be abhorred. In this general outlook, what is painful and what is evil seem ultimately to converge. Then again, how can we possibly respond to the radical question of why we should seek creative living/suffering? Perhaps there is a simple answer: we need it for the sake of our mind's survival. We need to recognise that the general problem of evil (in the sense of pain, anguish, misery) is a real one. Moreover, an essential part of being a person is the laborious combination of good and bad internal forces; an individual who primarily splits off and, therefore, obliterates the wickedness in himself is doomed to be largely a "nonperson". As we know, the person is often tempted to homogenise with whatever groups will allow him to drastically disown or deflect fearsome inner currents, even under the cover of meliorist, progressive ideals.

The story might go like this: no one would suffer from whatever ill effects (envy, hunger, shame, fatigue . . .) in a future, essentially different, society. After the Enlightenment, in the recent historical follies of right-wing or left-wing Hegelism, we nearly came to believe that continued social advancement would one day largely make emotional distress a thing of the past, an extinct illness. This omnipotent outlook radically departs from the guidelines of psychoanalysis, through which we learn that growth is rooted in innumerable small steps and very, very few great leaps. Creativity requires daily activity—which is not good news to many of us. It makes us responsible, while we tend to avoid just that. As if one were asking, "Do you really mean that I have to do something, such as carry out inner actions, in order to feel better?" Most of us dislike psychic actions when we can obsess instead on vast theoretical or explanatory considerations implying omnipotent conclusions. This attitude leads us to ask, "What is the use?" instead of creatively asking, "What is next?" Perhaps we can work with what we have rather than languish in complaints over what we do not have. A certain amount of labour is entailed in much sane, human transformation, and, by generally denying suffering, we are opposing much healthy growth.

We should also look at some side effects of our passive attitude. For instance, without painstakingly developing creative tools and a sufficient agentive attitude, some individuals will languish indefinitely in the wake of life's blows. Ashamed of our supposed lack of personality, secretive about grandiose dreams, we might channel our gifts into the most conformist arrangements, and forget our aspiration to struggle creatively at higher levels of commitment. I am, thus, trying to outline a framework that will help us to reveal the more positive aspects of suffering, and escape from languishing in passivity. These positive aspects are widely overlooked in a culture that devalues most forms of discomfort while simultaneously rhapsodising on every instance of happiness, irrespective of its particular depth, authenticity, or survival value (Davies, 2012, p. 113). Significantly, Maslow seems to attempt a synthesis when he remarks: "My feeling is that the concept of creativeness and the concept of the healthy, self-actualizing, fully human person seem to be coming closer and closer and may perhaps turn out to be the same things" (Maslow, 1968, p. 200). Yet, what we might call "bad faith" in our confrontation with different options will always demand some payment in our relationships. That is, in the burden that others will have to carry for us. According to Hollis, our children will possibly have to carry the consequences of our unlived life, of our uncreative suffering, in their own journeys (Hollis, 2003, p. 12). We may be driven by some automatic pilot when we settle for a passive, inertial attitude to adversity. A reversal of attitude requires an operational sense of self that will organise purposive energies of our psyche that have a propelling force, or a *telos*. "What does the soul ask of me?" seems to be a basic Jungian question. It certainly does not ask for the defences that tend to rule our life repetitively and, when unchallenged, put our lives on automatic pilot (Hollis, 2003, p. 12).

Of course, psychotropic drugs are a contemporary blessing, indeed, a most valuable clinical instrument. Still, as is often the case, it is a question of good or bad use. Unfortunately, the false assumption that intervening on the patient's biochemistry is in *every* case the best clinical strategy might prevail. In Davies' view, the danger is that by denying alternatives not only is a negative vision of suffering imposed, but also patients are virtually denied the maturational work through which a creative use of suffering can be made (Davies, 2012, p. 104). As an illustration, we could invoke an extreme example of a productive route for inner pain. The immensely creative irony of Kierkegaard is presented as a derivative of his suffering: "Since earliest childhood an arrow of grief has been buried in my heart. As long as it stays there I am ironic—if it is drawn out I'll die" (Kierkegaard,

1996, p. 268). If we could think of illness as of a living system falling apart, then the danger deriving from diverging routes could be better perceived. Our harmonising creativity no longer appears as a wishful psychic luxury, the celebrated desire for integration, but, rather, as a necessary, costly means of psychic evolution. Basically, it is the origin of mental agency, in contrast to passivity.

The question of agency and passivity

It seems that in Bion's view, creative suffering is our central psychic activity—our ultimate alchemy. He suggests that the patients for whom he attempts to formulate theories do experience pain, but do not really suffer.

> They may be suffering in the eyes of the analyst because the analyst can, and indeed must, suffer. The patient may say he suffers but this is only because he does not know what suffering is and mistakes feeling pain for suffering it . . . The intensity of the patient's pain contributes to his fear of suffering pain. (Bion, 1970, p. 19)

In his view, suffering pain involves respect for the experience of pain, one's own and another's. Such respect is not very common in the patient and, consequently, he has no respect for the procedures of psychoanalysis, a practice that is concerned with the existence of pain. Thus, pain can be inflicted or accepted without being creatively suffered. Indeed, a seminal outlook worthy of continued, assiduous attention.

In this connection, I would like to iterate that the divergent routes of agency (and creative suffering), on the one hand, and uncreative suffering (and passivity), on the other, are not just *alternative* paths because, in fact, they are also *alternating*, in a most challenging way. We can easily shift from one route to another. I shall, thus, try to tentatively explore these unavoidable, fearsome switches. As such, this section will not contribute a co-ordinated sequence of arguments, but, rather, an attempt to capture the intensity of these fluctuations.

The general idea is that inner pain, in whichever form, should not deaden us but should, instead, be used as a catalyst for our inner alchemy. Historically, alchemy was a process that required a seamless container (beaker, vessel, vase, crucible . . .) and very high temperatures to induce transformation: lead into gold, poison into medicine, etc. The procedures of alchemy are, of course, an appropriate metaphor for the illustration of analytic work: in fact it can *only* take place in a very tight and secure setting in which even exceptionally high emotional intensity can be generated and experienced. Conversely, pain that is not accurately processed could solidify into a paralysed "leaden heart" which makes any inner action difficult and allows only for primitive reactions, in contrast to psychic actions. This might, perhaps, sound like an impossible call to accept frustration, but it is not; it is "merely" the acceptance of an opportunity to actually see more of the situation before acting, to accept inner reality rather than be pulled into the vortex of reactions. The distinction between psychic actions and reactions is not proposed as an intellectual exercise. The art of creative complaint and the avoidance of reactive complaints are essential in the effort to break free from passivity—ultimately, inner paralysis. Paralysed subjects often tell themselves that they are either too old or too young, too inadequate, or too desperate to pursue meaningful transformative ventures, and that they can only react. The theories that we have in mind do not matter as much as the practice itself. Necessity, not theoretical virtue, is the beginning of our creative use of adversity. Our souls long for creative freedom, for meaning, and for connection. When this desire is intimidated by fear, rerouted by cultural idols, or projected on to others, something terrible can happen to our souls, such as carrying on in a mere parody of life.

The relevance of discouragement becomes clearer when we want to do something to relieve our pain, but we cannot because we feel hopeless. Paradoxically, success might even function in the same way, in as much as we fervently seek it as a means to be relieved from further struggle. Once we feel "successful", we become entitled to give up our personal agency because we become inclined to quasi-magical, quick-fix solutions. In this paradoxical sense, we could even say that success could damage our future emotional/developmental itinerary. Then again, inner passivity closely resembles psychic stupor and is ultimately deadening, and so the only serious psychological mistake we can make is not to do anything. In fact, we need a force strong enough to focus our concentration on one goal at a time, until we are finished with any of our micro-ventures. Lamenting complaint might even become a pastime. It is even becoming something of a fashionable leisure activity. However, it is not as innocent as we might think, for, essentially, it induces us to disregard the centrality of human suffering and to determine a blind spot on the question of inner pain—which is, indeed, an essential question.

On a philosophical level, it is puzzling that a great part of our scholarly contributions simply ignore the burning questions of our human distress. It is intellectually unjustified to believe that human knowledge, or knowledge of our knowing minds, can surpass or ignore all questions of suffering. On a more ordinary, informal level, our apparently mild and innocent daily complaints about tribulation seem to secretly introduce a perverse attitude of psychic sloth, ultimately conducive to our deadly affliction of passivity. As Baggini suggests, at the root of every complaint is a sense that things are not as they ought to be. To complain is to speak out against our predicament, and we can do so petulantly, aggressively, or mournfully (Baggini, 2010, p. 1). Apparently, some people are never happier than when they have an opportunity to complain. Yet, issues of human suffering cannot be detached from their most disparate expressions. Even accepting pain with muteness and rigidity can be a perverse way of complaining. In this sense, then, any expression of misery can be as challenging and consequential as misery itself. Under the worst political regimes, subjects may really loathe a particular policy, but the most that they can do is engage in passive resistance—which they have to disguise persistently. Inner persecutory regimes, or even family structures, can be no less oppressive and deadening: passivity is the ultimate price. Referring to her grandmother as someone who managed not to be reduced into a thing-like state, Chang writes, "Despite having lived a life of suffering and torment, her stories were not unbearable or depressing. Underlying them was a fortitude that was all the time uplifting" (Chang, 1991, p. 403). In this sense, her substantial expression of pain was somehow creative and certainly not perverse.

The seductive nature of passivity is more pervasive than we think. Even in psychoanalysis there is the temptation to accept a logic implying that since we have done our part, we must get the reward, and have earned our rest. This is a residue of a phantasmatic expectation to live an effort-free life and be exempted from all struggles. Once we have "done our part", we may erroneously believe that we can be excused from continuing efforts, almost as if success could become instrumental to passivity. Perhaps we all wish to reach some very special goal that will exempt us from subsequent efforts—an ultimately static condition. It almost looks like an infantile game; some variety of treasure hunt based on the assumption that once we find "it" we can resolve all of our problems and can relax into psychological inertia. The nature of the treasures ranges from a magic sword to the right theory, from a post of power to a recognition of genius. There is, of course, a great variety of minor but equally craved-for treasures which we use daily as stupefying anaesthetics.

The notion that one enters therapy in order to blame others (parental figures, especially) is enticing but deceptive. While we need to understand the character of our influential experiences and our consequent survival strategies, the ultimate point is to regain the captaincy of our journey. In Hollis's view, "If one has a modicum of consciousness and moral courage in the second half of life, then blame, if blame one must, is ours alone' (Hollis, 2003, p. 43). In a synthetic *aperçu* of Davies' work, we read, "I define as 'productive suffering' that which furthers our unfurling, while I define as 'unproductive suffering' that which hinders it" (Davies, 2012, pp. 6–7). And, of course, we can assess whether our suffering is creative primarily on the basis of whether it facilitates some kind of healthy change. Then again, this maturational creativity depends on our capacity to *endure* psychic distress. "Productive suffering is therefore an *active* state", concludes Davies (2012, p. 7). From a broader historical perspective, we could remark with Padoa-Schioppa that a tendency which has prevailed during the course of centuries cannot be changed in a moment (Padoa-Schioppa, 2006, p. 6). It is, therefore, most dangerous to give historical events only one chance. History demands repeated opportunities. The worst enemies of human advances are those who are impatient and those who are disenchanted. Under Padoa-Schioppa's gaze, they seem to say, "I really tried, I believed in it more than anyone else; I am therefore entitled to affirm that the dream of a political union is an illusion" (2006, p. 6, translated for this edition). He claims that this is a slothful kind of patience, that it is a passive, lamenting, and ultimately perverse form of wisdom.

In Ferro's work on emotions, he argues that the avoidance of emotions is one of the main activities of our mind, however exhausting and uncreative. This troublesome avoidance of emotions is as problematic as the indigestible emotions that must be expelled. In his view, even the "miniaturisation of emotions" ultimately serves "the avoidance of emotional impacts which would otherwise be impossible to manage" (Ferro, 2011, p. 1). To further illustrate his thesis, he says that, "We can evacuate into the body of the individual in the form of psychosomatic illness or into the social body in such forms as character disorders, criminality and *collective stupidity*" (Ferro, 2011, p. 1): stupidity in the sense of *stupor*. Our abhorrence of difficult emotions can indeed be evacuated in "collective stupidity", such as, for instance, in our smile-or-die culture. Alumni journals of prestigious universities invariably feature smiling figures to confirm to former students that they did receive the very best education. In this way, they also attract prospective students in the direction of successful "winners" and towards the "right" choice. In Ferro's outlook, we could say that our compulsory smiles (our "collective stupidity") might be the reply to our incapacity to confront and utilise our primitive, stony, painful emotions. The smile-or-die attitude seems to discourage, or even forbid, any contact with psychic suffering. They may even teach *happiness* courses in prestigious universities, while not being able to teach the use of misery. Indeed, billions are invested by our best minds for achieving or selling success, which is supposed to be the specific antidote of suffering.

Significantly, Phillips includes on the same page in his book *Winnicott*: (a) the suggestion that psychotherapy can be viewed as a form of playing together with a "marked preference for open-ended games in which play is not circumscribed by agreed-upon rules", and (b) the mention of a patient carrying a revolver (Phillips, 1988, p. 15). But, of course, when revolvers and bullets are involved, we cannot easily engage in any sort of open-ended games.

Only Winnicott could have honestly and candidly inserted this footnote to his argument, "When the analyst knows that the patient carries a revolver, then, it seems to me, this work cannot be done' (Winnicott, 1971, quoted in Phillips, 1988, p. 14). Yet, there can be psychic revolvers in *any* analysis and revolvers can be alternatively directed to either one in the dyad. All of this coincides with Ferro's analytic approach where he actually says, "It should be easy to think of 'bullets' in terms of aggressiveness, whereas to me they are *explosive protoemotional states* on the point of being evacuated, awaiting only the mental readiness of the other to find a place where they can be contained and transformed: (Ferro, 2011, p. 4). Ferro thinks of bullets as indicating hard, pointed, dangerous, sensorial aspects of the psyche, to be dealt with and processed so that they can be diverted into alternative, creative currents. When these primitive elements are not included, we incline to believe that the therapy is not sufficiently deep, or realistic. We could say that the celebrated "pure gold" of analysis can only be alchemically attained through the capacity to endure the distress, pain indeed, of dealing with relational bullets in a sufficiently good "combustion chamber".

Normally, we envision peace of mind as a resting place or as some absence of pain. Perhaps such a situation is not one of peace but, rather, of benumbing passivity. Because it requires constant work to stay connected with one's entire self (which includes "explosive protoemotional states", psychic revolvers, and bullets), real peace of mind must be an active condition, involving constant agentive work. If there is no such thing as life *without* pain, we can only use it to the best. As an illustrative analogy, we could say that immense quantities of energy can be derived from the forces of nature (sun, sea, winds, etc.) but require that we labour to process and channel them. Energy does not simply flow into our homes; it requires agency to harvest it. Yet, we cannot simply say that we should choose between creative and uncreative suffering because we simply do not make a choice of what seems best. Why? Because we are predominantly inclined to *avoid* difficult emotions, even if we can glimpse their creative potential (Davies, 2012, p. 112). Our inner routes are not simply alternatives from which to choose, for they are also alternating routes. It is a matter of fluctuations that we have to monitor and endure. The onset of our engagement with creative suffering might even strike us in the form of a sudden onset of depression (Why should there be such eruptions of explosive, protoemotional elements in the therapy *I* conduct? Perhaps I am inadequate or insufficiently competent?), the occurrence of anxiety (What will become of the patient and of myself? What will "they" say?), or a sudden fear of loss (Will he opt out of analysis? What will he do to me? What can I do then?). In a synoptic outlook, Davies suggests that we should see the onset of suffering more as an opportunity for renewal than as the hallmark of personal affliction. This view implies that anaesthetising our suffering precipitously might impede the revitalisation that entering creative suffering may entail (Davies, 2012, p. 112). Blocked patients or analysts are, in general, not lazy people: they are just stuck. Being blocked is quite different from being slothful. The blocked individual typically expends a great deal of inner energy, although not in a visible way. The deadened, stupefied individual never knows how to take the first uncertain steps. He might be obsessed with frightening, grandiose, impossible tasks that are totally uncreative. The frequent hours of analytic therapy seem primarily to teach us a method of innumerable small steps, one after the other.

CHAPTER TWO

Psychic anaesthetics

Sara and her drugs: resisting anaesthesia

This is not a proper clinical presentation but, rather, a tentative segment of psychobiography, provided for the purpose of illustrating the possible long-term vicissitudes of inner pain. I met Sara in a state psychiatric hospital three years *before* she came to me for analysis. In the psychiatric ward, she was heard demanding psychoanalytic therapy while being looked at with compassion for believing that some "talking cure" could produce the same effects as major psychotropic drugs. She was told that people in her condition needed medication, and was given massive amounts of drugs. She kept saying that she was feeling unreal, like a zombie. Several years after her various hospitalisations, she revealed in analysis that her "personal spirit" had been with her throughout her psychotic years, and that she was attentive to what was happening but powerless to let herself become known. Her analysis lasted eleven years, with sessions three times per week.

The matter-of-course statements and tone of dismissal with which they treated what, to her, were the most crushing pains, the most frightening thoughts, were easily accounted for in terms of psychiatric problems, also related to her mother's condition: she was a chronic delusional person. She could certainly be ill, but definitely she could not have personal, *painful* problems. After somehow finishing high school, she experienced all her deep-seated archaic emotions rising to tumultuous activity and she was faced with frightening dilemmas. Where should she go? What could she do? She realised with terror that her mind was continually sliding into inward suppressed rage, lethargy, and confusion. She kept taking drugs that made her feel deadened and sad. The attitude of haste and worry in her family tended to coincide with the psychiatric approach: if there are problems or difficulties, these must be pathological mental problems to be promptly treated and cured by medicines, so that she would not have to suffer so much. Family care amounted to her being taken to different, frequent psychiatric consultations and even occasional hospitalisations in private hospitals. Her mother was a "quiet" delusional person and, of course, her daughter had to have problems comparable to those of her poor mother. Whenever Sara went to see a psychiatrist she took along a shoebox full of all the medicines that she was constantly urged to take. She raged about not being able to *live* her own suffering, about not feeling it to the full, and to see *through* it. Paradoxically, she seemed to need drugs to keep going, while loathing them for making her feel numb and flattened. She floundered among incongruities and was left to herself, while her elders went about organising treatment.

Sara was younger than her two brothers and, in the course of her analysis, often spoke of their sexually abusive behaviour. It was not that they forced her to have intercourse, for it was mostly a question of frequent sexual harassing, which they perpetrated both individually and together and also joked about in public. Her father was a military man and was irascible most of the time. Sara's mother often heard "voices" and felt persecuted by envious neighbours; she took medicication and lived as a rather quiet, amiable person. Sara somehow felt responsible for her mother because she was the sort of person "who can become very easily confused". She had to protect her so that she might provide a minimum of maternal care. She had to defend herself from her father's rage and from her brothers' abuse in order to try not to burden her mother with excessive problems. Added to this, she lost a twin sister in her first year of life and was made to feel guilty for her death.

At the beginning of her analysis, it was primarily a question of repossessing her suffering so that she could use it for her own development. She secretly resented being psychically anaesthetised to the point that she often talked about living like a zombie and felt that she could only throw her dead weight upon me, hoping that I could endure it.

She presented me with multiple painful and enraging scenarios in which she narrated over and over again a basic story a superabundance of wild, primitive emotions that she was unable to cope with by means of transformations, and which she evacuated through a variety of symptoms. Alternatively, she let herself become dumbed and flattened by drugs. She was asking to *personally* think of these alternatives together, so that she could generate something creative for her own self, rather than be reduced to a thing-like state by drugs. In the course of her first two years of analysis, she gradually "forgot" to take medicines and eventually became entirely drug-free.

Not knowing what to do with herself, she enrolled in a five-year programme in psychology at the local state university. Fees were nominal and she would, thus, have somewhere to go. She assiduously attended courses, participated in all seminars and study groups, and felt increasingly welcome and accepted. Studying her books in her free time at first functioned as a way to avoid her thoughts. At the same time, in the course of her first three years of college, she was introduced to a powerful, leftist, extra-parliamentary group that then developed into the terrorist movement known as the Red Brigades. Her interest was genuine and enthusiastic; she was increasingly appreciated and "instructed". In the end, however, when she was about to be definitely recruited, she opted out of the group because she did not feel entirely convinced by the programme. Of course, we deeply elaborated her choice to do this in analysis. Perhaps, in the end, she decided to refuse the ultimate form of anaesthesia: homogenising into a powerful, salvational ideology—even though it was that of a terrorist group. She was then expelled from the highly supportive group, and was left alone with her own paradoxes, which she finally accepted for the purpose of repossessing her own life. She was still afraid of "ghosts" in her family. Her sense of hopelessness had previously increased to the point that she could not help herself. She could only break the nightmare by displaying psychiatric symptoms.

Everything was painful, highly charged, and offensive in her home life: her older abusive brothers even joked about her avoidant responses. Although she was a pretty girl, her self-loathing had deepened and her self-esteem had collapsed: she dressed in the worst possible way with hardly any awareness of doing so. As is known, a child who, from its earliest years, is certain that her attachment figures will be available when she needs them will develop a sense of security and inner confidence. In adult life, this confidence would make it possible for her to trust and love other human beings. But Sara had hardly experienced any of that. Yet, she had to protect her mother—and even her entire family. Sara was seen as being good at recognising everyone else's needs, but deprived of sufficiently good experiences of being recognised herself. And so her "project" was to fit in with whatever her elders wanted her to be, or what she imagined they wanted.

One of the relevant aspects of her analysis was her re-experiencing her childhood despair about the impossibility of her personal gifts being valued. She was quite certain that not even a psychoanalyst could have a feeling for that. No one in her family had a college education and even her enrolment at the state university was looked upon with irony and disapproval. Her elders could only value activities within the boundaries of their own sphere of ambition. Even if, by chance, their hopes for her had coincided with a field in which she could be successful, they would have been quite unable to mirror for her those specific, real attributes that could result in excellence. The capacities that were the result of her creativity were manifested in subtle ways, quite different from the obvious superiority of the more acclaimed students. As a consequence, she initially viewed her awareness that she understood psychology better than others did as a dangerous delusion. The utilisation of her capacities in her field of study was never even contemplated until she was noticed by a few perceptive professors, who encouraged her. The sense of being crazy rather than gifted persisted for a while in the form of constant uncertainties about the quality of her work, in spite of the acknowledgement it received from her teachers. Sometimes, she pulled herself together almost beyond capacity, beyond courage, when she had to endure confrontations in seminars and in her "training" within the ultra-leftist group. She developed almost an overemphasis on integration, not allowing herself enough time to let herself go astray spontaneously and eventually come together again in a few days, as if everything had to move at a high speed and under pressure. With boys, she had learnt to surrender herself to them superficially, while remaining deeply invisible and perhaps defiant. Being a star in college was one thing and dealing with her innermost self was another. Were both possible? Could they enhance each other? Sara strenuously worked at her analysis and almost never missed a session in the course of eleven years. She managed to come in spite of transportation strikes, heavy snowfalls, and torrential rain that soaked her completely.

In order to get where she was, Sara had to re-feel and mourn the wounding she had endured as a young child and adolescent coping with her abusive brothers, the "memory" of a lost twin sister, a most fragile mother, and a constantly irascible father. She had to make her peace with those apparently lost years. But revisiting her pathology without any anaesthetics and being fully alive was also fearsome. In her college years, no one wanted to pay any attention to the shaky, crying part of her successful self—not even the best and most perceptive of her professors. They wanted only that "beautiful mind" and interesting person to function well. They listened to her negative parts just enough to rationalise them away, while the successful part was pushed to shine on stage. Of course, there were excluded, neglected areas that would not go away and which we had to absorb again and again in analysis—with no anaesthetics. Her blocked family found her recovery disturbing. Her becoming unblocked raised the unsettling possibility that they, too, could become unblocked and move towards the risk of authentic suffering rather than remain in the slough of cynicism, delusion, or rage. Indeed, as castrated, abject minds, they found her recovery unbearable. Their constant doubts often reactivated Sara's own. They were somehow trying to lever her back into old ways for the sake of retaining her comfort and company. Sadly, one of her brothers committed suicide.

Sara finally graduated with honours and a few options opened for her. After two years, Sara was given a six-months contract with the state hospital for chronic psychiatric patients. Her job also involved residing for two months in a holiday location in the hills of Rome, where the patients could have a holiday while the premises of the state hospital were being upgraded. She was responsible for organising their daily schedule and for administering medication, in which she was assisted by two psychiatric nurses, both men. She kept the patients busy all day with walks in the countryside, choral singing, group dancing, card games, cooking, jokes, and contests. Everything went very well, and the experience was most encouraging for her. She told me about the vicissitudes of her working summer at the beginning of September, when we resumed analysis. She also explained, to my increasing horror, that after about two weeks she simply stopped giving the patients their drugs. Of course, this could be seen as dangerous acting out, as irresponsible behaviour, as lack of professional ethics. Perhaps she omnipotently used her story to attribute it to others. As she became able to endure her own pain and do without drugs, she somehow transferred the experience on to others. The senior psychiatrist to whom she reported the events at the end of the sojourn reprimanded her severely, but said that he would not denounce her because he did not want to ruin her career, and also because there had been no accidents. I was very concerned about the whole story, but she "explained" to me that everything was going very well with the patients, and that she just did not have the heart to give them *"quelle schifezze"*—those useless, loathsome things. Of course, extensive work was done as a consequence of the summer experience. Sara concluded her analysis after eleven years of work. She found a good job as a civil servant, and never again worked as a psychologist. When we terminated analysis, she was newly married and about to move to another city.

From temporary to permanent

As a way of introducing the problem of our relentless quest for anaesthetics, we could quote from Lewis's work:

> When I think of pain, of anxiety that gnaws like fire and loneliness that spreads out like a desert, and the heartbreaking routine of monotonous misery, or again of dull aches that blacken our whole landscape, or sudden nauseating pains that knock a man's heart out at one blow, of pains that seem already intolerable and then are suddenly increased, of infuriating scorpion-sting pains that startle into maniacal movement a man who seemed half dead with previous tortures—it quite overcrows my spirit. (Lewis, 2012, p. 105)

He also says that if he knew any way of escape he would "crawl through sewers" to find it. "But what is the good of telling you about my feelings?" he concludes, "You know them already: they are the same as yours" (Lewis, 2012, p. 105). What we can try to demonstrate is that we constantly seek the most disparate and costly ways of anaesthetising these inner pains. No human ingenuity is left unexplored for the relief of psychic pain. As is known, Freud himself was an example of this quest. For the sake of illustration, let us just name at random some of our contemporary anaesthetics: alcohol or ideologies, psychotropic drugs or consumption of goods, substance addiction or search for power. The consequent problem, though, is that the anaesthetics we select might not remain simply temporary remedies. As we shall see, the truth is that they tend to become permanent. In fact, our so-called repetition compulsion ultimately works for better or worse in all of our ventures. The common phobia of distress and suffering, together with the desperate search for ever-new anaesthetisers, can be regarded as serious impediments to our human spontaneity. It is interesting that learning to suffer sufficiently well, or even creatively, is a precursor to a full psychic life and that the "act" of suffering can be more enriching than anaesthetised indifference. This inconspicuous capacity can be the source of psychic strength and health. In the view of Hesse, a part of our self seems to dictate that pain is just pain, that it obviously hurts and no compromise is possible; there are remedies that can defeat frustration and these are weapons that can be acquired and successfully used; it would be madness if you would accept suffering (Hesse, 1997, p. 45). Another deeper, subtler voice, however, might seem to suggest something like this: pain is hurtful only because you fear it so much; it stalks you precisely because you constantly try to avoid it. The most hurtful feature of inner pain is your dislike of it; it is this refusal that makes pain so painful and in need of being anaesthetised (Hesse, 1997, p. 45). Even though the first voice has reason on its side and, thus, sounds more immediately convincing, ultimately, we damage ourselves by fostering incompatibility with pain. The conflict of these two voices can be psychically consuming. But then, in a synthetic *aperçu*, we could say that each voice is, to some extent, contaminated by the desire of the contrary, antagonistic voice. The desire to avoid pain can, in fact, be influenced by the desire to endure it for the sake of using it. On the other hand, the desire to accept pain is influenced by the desire to ultimately overcome it.

Indeed, the avoidance of pain marks our personal itinerary from its very beginning. Perhaps humans as a species have spoiled themselves, and, thus, wellbeing in our present state must mean primarily remedial or corrective anaesthesia. What is significant in self-formation is that what might feel like an effective temporary anaesthetic tends to metamorphose into a stable attitude and, furthermore, is an attitude of which we are either not aware or try to ignore. Some of us might try to eliminate fathers and conquer mothers, to destroy external enemies, to avoid thinking and opt for outer actions, but then, all of these choices are derived from our incapacity to endure some psychic labour and, thus, they ultimately function as anaesthetics. We might not resist inside our cluttered mental room and, thus, might look avidly for outer trouble to defeat, in the erroneous belief that it will alleviate our unbearable inner condition. Freud "counsels" to avoid parricide and opt for negotiation; Klein urges us to avoid schizo-paranoid ventures and endure depressive states; Bion exhorts us to opt for thinking rather than unthoughtful acting; Jung insists that we should not part from our shadowy self in search of some superhuman, painless condition. However, all of these options require from us a measure of patience, endurance, and tolerance. The real poor of the world are those who cannot afford any anguish, as if it were an unapproachable monster, which it is not, after all. From our psychoanalytic perspective, development largely depends on the relative success in tolerating the coexistence of love and hatred—which are often kept apart at any cost. In his *Winnicott* book, Phillips reminds us that the developing infant

> splits the mother into good and bad parts . . . The two parts never meet in his mind for fear of consequences. With the depressive position comes the idea of the mother as a whole person commensurate with but also distinct from the infant's existence. At this point the depressive position comes to the fore. (Phillips, 1988, p. 56)

In addition, our relentless search of palliatives comes to the fore. Segal states it thus: "At this stage the defences are directed against experiencing the psychic reality of the depressive pain, and their main characteristic is a denial of psychic reality" (Segal, 1989, p. 81). This would be the ultimate, perfect anaesthetic. How is that for a solution? To attempt a synthesis of our constant inclination to anesthetise pain, we could say with Phillips, "By the use of the manic defence the individual is emotionally impoverished but apparently protected from what is felt to be intolerable pain" (Phillips, 1988, p. 57). The infant has to tolerate the guilt and anxiety (that is, inner pain) that arise from concern about having injured a person he loves, and this brings with it "new defences to deal with a new kind of pain" (Phillips, 1988, p. 57). As we know, Klein's depressive position was meant, in her view, to replace the centrality Freud had accorded to the Oedipus complex. In fact Klein places psychic distress—fear, guilt, anxiety—at the centre of human development. Ultimately, many of our human pleasures become implicitly represented as ways of alleviating those psychic states.

There is also an insidious hindrance to our self-directed learning from experience, one that makes growth and creativity more difficult than they should be. It is a barrier that might, if surmounted, lead to dead ends: this is our obstinate ignorance of having problems with psychic pain. This is a problem that needs to be rendered conspicuous and recognised. If we can become relatively familiar with it, we will not have to resort to the pre-emptive use of remedial anaesthetics. According to Davies, "Much emotional suffering will be simply prolonged or even rendered unproductive by its not being allowed to reach its full depth . . . taste enough of the medicine of suffering to recoil, but never enough to recover" (Davies, 2012, p. 156). Our markets thrive on this pervasive need for mitigating human misery. We hear that the era of market triumphalism has come to an end. Has it really? Where can we try to acquire the desirability and prestige that we presume will provide friends and alleviate the pain of solitude? Where can we buy instruments for self-esteem and co-option by the "best"?' How can we induce peace of mind and so relax? Of course, low self-esteem, loneliness, exclusion, and anxiety are all aspects of our human condition. We live in a time in which we can easily believe that almost anything can be bought and sold. In our financial times, markets and market values have come to govern our lives as never before. We did not arrive at this stage through any deliberate choice. It is almost as if it came upon us imperceptibly (Sandel, 2012, p. 5). We should also remark, with Haybron, that human beings are systematically prone to make a wide range of serious errors in matters of personal welfare (Haybron, 2010, p. 227). These errors are serious enough to substantially compromise the expected lifetime well-being for individuals possessing a high degree of freedom to shape their lives as they wish. Why should these individuals incur so much inner pain? How well equipped are we to *benefit* from certain freedoms?

With all the qualifiers, we still recognise that pleasure is one of the central "goods" in life. Suffering, conversely, is one of the central evils. Any theory that cannot make sense of such platitudes has a lot of explaining to do. Likewise, suffering is bad because of what it is *like* to suffer (Haybron, 2010, p. 165). Actually, this attitude appears to have come upon us because we remain ignorant of inner pain and try to fight our misery prevalently by means of anaesthetic instruments, which constitute a large part of the whole global market. We do not want knowledge; we want anaesthesia. We could say, with Sandel, that most consumer purchases are attempts at exorcising psychic pain (Sandel, 2012, p. 5). Just think of food and drink, and even of theories and ideologies.

Davies explores in depth the social and individual consequences of avoiding creative suffering. When we avoid a confrontation with our primary conflicts, we become prone to enter a stagnant condition, one in which both aggressive impulses and libidinal energies are no longer called into action. As is known, the "rigidity" that can impede a psychoanalytic process in many subtle ways is commonly called "resistance", which is the defensive habit by which we eschew certain uncomfortable insights about ourselves (Davies, 2012, p. 91). As is known, patients might even cling to their invalidating pathology rather than attempt the necessary steps required to transform the situation. As Freud believed, our defence mechanisms are an expression of that part of us that wishes to return to an alleged infantile condition of unconsciousness and dependence. At the onset of our attempts to enter creative suffering, we may experience a sense of personal loss and failure. The distress frequently encountered in our times presents more opportunities for learning from experience than our pharmaceutical industries currently recognise or allow for (Davies, 2012, p. 112). Paradoxically, when the need for psychic anaesthesia is overwhelming, we come even to prefer a deadened condition to a tempestuous inner life. By way of example, we could invoke an enlightening interpretation pertaining to the well known "weekend frustration". Grotstein dares to say to a patient, "You were hungry for anaesthesia, not hungry for nurture. You were hungry for anaesthesia against ungratified neediness because of your feeling unable to take care of yourself on your own" (Grotstein, 2009, p. 174).

At the opposite end of extreme defences, we have a perfect cover—the obliteration of pain. For this, we refer to Bion's clinical acumen:

> We can become callous to the actual nature of the pain . . . I know from my own experience that one loses sight of the fact that the patient is suffering—and you are helped by the patient to lose sight of that. A patient may be so "amusing" that the session is quite enjoyable; *it seems almost unkind to remember that the patient has come because he is suffering*. (Bion, 2005, p. 5, my emphasis)

Yes, indeed, perhaps we need to remember that patients do suffer.

At the exact opposite of a deadened condition there is the extreme analgesic of falling in love. Being in love is generally regarded as the elixir of life. Of course, love comes in myriad varieties, but there is one particular type of amorous experience that often functions as an immediate anaesthetic; it is the rapture of a nearly magical state of mind and heart that entirely possesses the person (Yalom, 2011, p. 208). Certainly, we should be greatly appreciative of those who are in love and for whom what was just a world suddenly becomes a star. This is a blessing, as long as one is not imprisoned or paralysed by the passionate condition. If we are suddenly and madly in love, the pursuit of truth might even seem threatening. We do not want to interfere with the fragile and shiny condition of our "happiness". We want to stay lost in the sea of bliss rather than be reminded that there is an "I" in the me (or an "eye" in the we) that is temporarily blinded. Being in love in a "sick" way might even be an attempt to alleviate a transgenerational problem. Real life lived daily in a creative way is perceived as a compromise, and the adjustment can be seen as a betrayal of the ideal, oceanic feeling of being in love. We are creative in our daily contact with our world—the relational situation that obtains—and do not despise it just because being in love changes what is just a world into a star. In a "sick" way, should a loved person become available, we are tempted to abandon that person because he or she is no longer the locus of our idealising projections. We could perhaps think of a mature form of being in love, in the sense of love for the unity with, and the destiny of, the partner. In fact, we can hardly make a list of our anaesthetising routes for which we ordinarily think that the admission price is never too high. *Au dessus d'un certain prix, il n'y a plus de prix*. (Above a certain price, there is no price.) Perhaps we should not forget a frequent transmutation of falling in love—that is, the experience of love obsession. With regard to analgesic devices, we might even think that the love obsession could serve as a screen, keeping the enamoured person from more challenging thoughts. We could even ask what he would be thinking about if he were not obsessed with that (Yalom, 2011, p. 208), and perhaps the celebrated "romantic love" could be a milder form of quasi-obsessive love. What is unique about it is that it upholds an array of redemptive features that ultimately function as analgesics. Davies lists several characteristics of romantic love, such as, "Romantic love is always salvational and redemptive"; "Romantic love will solve all problems, enrich the personality and endow life with perpetual meaning"; "Romantic love is a remedy for all ills" (Davies, 2012, pp. 78–79). He reminds us that to deny romantic love might be regarded as sacrilegious, and that those who do so are considered unfeeling and incomplete (Davies, 2012, p. 80).

Familiarity with inner pain

If we can gain a more intense familiarity with psychic suffering we could attempt a *creative* coexistence with it. If we do not develop this familiarity we can become almost phobic about pain and vulnerable to succumbing to virtually any form of analgesic—even the most dangerous ones. We need to become conversant with distress so that we do not *automatically* lapse into the use of anaesthetics. In Bion's view, pain is a fact of existence, and not so very different from pleasure; we require a terminology in which there are no specific words so much as concrescences: "A number of feelings or ideas get collected together and could be put into some sort of order. You could regard pleasure and pain as different ends of the spectrum" (Bion, 2005, p. 5). There are many aspects to our relative familiarity with pain. In fact, it is quite easy to see why we like to have a nice feeling and even to believe that it is possible to entertain such a feeling by itself. However, this is rubbish, in Bion's view:

> You have to suppose that either you have feelings or you don't. If you are not willing to pay the price for the inescapable fact of pain, then you get reduced to a situation in which you try to isolate yourself. Physically, it is quite possible . . . Mentally, I don't think it is quite so easy. (Bion, 2005, p. 5)

Of course, the worst possible isolation is the detachment from our own self. The imposed centrifugal power of a benumbing culture seems utterly opposed to the creativity so strongly advocated by

Winnicott. A culture that pushes us into so-called internal "comfort zones", or compartments, seems to intimate that there cannot be (creative) suffering in the individual and that the *real* creative thought can only be found in whatever is the dominant intellectual élite—no matter how insane that might be. Through constant deviation from what is personal (and suffering is primarily very personal) to what is socially advertised and offered as a remedy, in fact an analgesic, one is ultimately deprived of instruments for enhancing one's inner life. The basic malignant message is, "Don't be so foolish as to struggle to make sense of your suffering: just use any of the plentiful remedies." And that is it. This is so popular that it is becoming a social mantra.

The avoidance of pain is the key to our ever-growing markets. Perhaps no other mechanism, the principle for organising the production and distribution of goods, has proved as successful at generating affluence and prosperity (Sandel, 2012, pp. 5–6). Yet, even as growing numbers of countries around the world embrace market mechanisms in the operation of their economies, something else is also happening. Market values are coming to play a greater and greater role in our cultural life. The economy of the avoidance of pain is now becoming dominant. Today, the logic of buying and selling no longer applies only to material goods, but increasingly governs our whole life. Theories, priorities, epistemic spaces, psychic, spiritual, and mental goods are all on the market. It is time to ask whether we want to live that way. I think that the question could be framed in these terms: it is time to ask whether we can afford *not* to live in this way. We need to find out whether or not we can advance to a different, more centripetal view. As we spend most of our resources trying to enhance individual or collective self-esteem, heal our inner wounds, buy peace of mind, exorcise our fear of death, and acquire some meaning to life (ideologies, in fact, sell just that), we should perhaps reassess the wisdom of these investments. Much of what passes for modern culture, as Pascal noted even in the seventeenth century, is a vast *divertissement* away from suffering; it results in even more misery as it estranges us from the deeper encounter with our individual journey (Pascal, 1995, p. 1).

Why suffer for not being among the best—the best in every sense? How could we suffer again the pangs of inadequacy if we have earned a written document that proves the exact opposite and provides for interlocking relations always ready to confirm it? Me ugly? For heaven's sake! This certificate says *Miss America*! There seems to be a delusional coalition to make us crave the very best of educational institutions, and this collective illusion usually involves very high costs. If you can make others believe that an institution is the best source of superior higher education, really of multi-faceted brilliance, people will do anything to avail themselves of its services. The other side of the illusion is the threat that you can suffer a great deal if you are not situated among the so-called "best". Probably it does not really matter which college we go to; what truly matters is how well we can take advantage of whatever its assets are. The same is probably true in the choice of a psychoanalyst. Once we are made to believe that we have had the best education in the very best place, we automatically believe that others will believe that, too—and perhaps they will. The same could be true when one is in search of some superstar psychoanalyst. This perverse magic becomes unstoppable. Such an outlook is so widespread that to call it insane seems to violate the definition of the word.

Unlike physical analgesics, psychic anaesthetics are not so innocently temporary. They might have a tendency to become addictive and, thus, become coextensive to our inner world. Then we may summon all of our strategies of anaesthetised living in order to create a barrier to inner pain—a rampart easily swamped by the onslaught of any tide of unhappy events (Davies, 2012, p. 146). All of our anaesthetising devices can easily collapse. There is no final answer, and there are many false paths to recovery (such as the analgesic remedies). We should be determined not to tread upon those paths. We risk becoming incapable of inner actions (in contrast to reactions), and opting constantly for external actions such as eliminating an archenemy or ingesting a remedy—from the forbidden fruit in the Garden of Eden to very particular substances. Addictions perhaps do just that. From a different, ulterior perspective, we could even say that addictive thinking is one of the derivatives of the oracular voices that we have passively absorbed to relieve distress, voices that may invade us in the form of mind-scripts on which we constantly elaborate.

It is interesting to note that we do not give oracles or analgesics indiscriminately to the persons we truly care for, but even "love" can be uncaring. Of course, there is kindness in love, but love and kindness are not necessarily convergent. In fact, when kindness is separated from the other elements of love, it involves a certain inconspicuous indifference to its object, and even something like condescendence. Kindness, on its own, cares not whether the other becomes better or worse, provided only that he escapes suffering. In Lewis's view, it is for people whom we care nothing about that we demand happiness on any terms: with those who are dear to us we are more exacting, and would rather see them struggling than be happy in contemptible and estranging ways (Lewis, 2012, p. 106). At our best, we would like to persuade those we love to become interested in the problem, and not fascinated by any apparently instant solution. In fact, we advocate familiarity with the problem. Speaking of the professional magician Houdini, what Phillips called his "escape claws" actually amounted to moments of blindness (Phillips, 2002, p. 21). The self-cure that Houdini had found for his restlessness was more like a drink to an alcoholic.

What we are affirming, then, is that since creative suffering can facilitate consciousness, by steadily anaesthetising our pain we may hinder the process of becoming lucidly familiar with our inner misery. Drawing together converging remarks, we may recognise, with Davies, that developing greater consciousness involves an increasing endurance of suffering. In Davies' words, "Much consciousness arises out of productive suffering. This is not to say, however, that all suffering produces consciousness, for . . . there is what I have called unproductive suffering" (Davies, 2012, pp. 129–130). This accompanies our psychic symptoms, which move us nowhere, and add nothing of value to our lives. Davies adds that this is not to say that consciousness can be attained *only* through suffering; in fact, consciousness can also develop through enlightening, intense experiences (Davies. 2012, p. 130). A person who succeeds in significantly helping another may discover in the process his inner empathy and strength. What Davies calls "unproductive suffering" presents another important feature: it is essentially passive, and a derivative of our incapacity to identify the primary problem at the root of the symptomatic condition (Davies, 2012, p. 72). From a psychoanalytic perspective, a person afflicted by any variety of symptoms may gradually struggle to uncover the primary weakness, or the primitive non-mentalized components of his condition, as a route to a very creative path. Davies insists that productive suffering, unlike unproductive suffering, consists in our confrontation with a deeper obstacle that sits behind, and is responsible for, the secondary problem. "Anaesthetic regimes", he concludes, "predominantly address themselves *to the unproductive suffering that attends our secondary problems*. In other words, they have no interest in helping people *suffer productively*" (Davies, 2012, p. 72, my emphasis). This is significant: unless you know the basic mechanisms behind the working of any clever analgesic regime, you will not recognise it, and it will trick you into adhering to it again and again. This means it takes you over, like a talented impostor, pretending to be who you are. Also, the act of recognition itself is one of the ways in which awakening happens and endurance develops. In fact, if we have a drastic aversion to not being liked, to not having our egos pleasantly stroked, we might even degrade our interactions into caricatures. How can we get our neighbours to like us? The chances are that we learn to become clever and proficient in twisting and turning in the solicitation of "approval" if the lack of approval proves too painful. This approval seeking is often at work in our pathological relations. In our psychoanalytic jargon, we constantly talk about infinitely diversified clinical conditions. Perhaps what they have in common is that they hurt—both patient and therapist. Thus, we would rather utilise the pain than anaesthetise it and make the situation even more passively deadening. The process of gaining familiarity with our inner suffering ultimately tells us that we can be the real protagonists.

The role of ideologies

There is no limit to the devices that we use to mitigate our suffering. When anaesthetics relieve our distress, they also silence any messages our suffering is trying to communicate. As is known, we use analgesics in an inverse proportion to our tolerance of pain; the less the tolerance, the greater the use of drug-like anaesthetics. Paradoxically, this crucial clinical–social issue appears largely ignored. The experience of our suffering becomes significant indeed, as it signals that certain adverse social or psychological conditions are holding us back. In fact, the most powerful ideologies—the "successful" ones—tend to neutralise our experience of suffering and, thus, function as effective anaesthetics that are especially ministered to the less fortunate, to the "poor". Perhaps they are not just ministered to us for, in fact, we might assiduously seek them for the purpose of reorganising our inner lives. Such is our human condition: for the sake of avoiding pain we actually become "lost in thoughts". What kind of thoughts? The kind generated by a collective cluster of beliefs that promises salvation and coherence. No price is too high for the promise of a unifying view of self and world. Just a cursory look at the past century will testify that we can easily entrust the full responsibility of our inner coherence, and resolution of suffering, to external agencies offering redemption, emancipation—and anaesthesia. These thoughts tell us that we cannot reach a glorified "there" from our abject "here" unless we find the conglomeration of thoughts that is requisite for the fateful move. The anaesthetic function of these thoughts is so powerful that we might even risk/offer our life, once it has been homogenised by a salvational ideology. A glimpse of insight may break the spell occasionally. Thus, paradoxically, things may get worse and better at the same time. Our stream of thoughts might have such an enormous momentum that it can easily drag us along. It is very easy for us to become immured in a pathological, rationalistic prison.

Fundamentalism, whether it is religious, political, or psychological, is a flight from adulthood and appeals to many because life is so difficult. If I can find some ideology that can rationalise the suffering of life for me, then I will have to buy into it. Such ideological happiness—even when it is attainable—is a manifestation of our weakest part of the self for it is based on the avoidance of the enigmatic challenge of any journey. Thinking is no longer adaptive or productive (let alone creative) when it is reduced to an addiction. Theory, likewise, is no longer theoretical—and inclines to ideology—when it loses sight of its conditional nature and circulates constantly as a form of epistemic inquisition. Some people manage to not be dominated by this oppressive use of thinking and rethinking about oracular voices. Perhaps every addiction arises from an unconscious refusal to face and move through our pain, however "moderate" it may be. For those who want certainty, let them find a group of like-minded people, make an ideological pledge, and make final decisions. The pledge will have no bearing on reality, of course. The overbearing dogmatism of the situation will reveal/conceal only the anxiety that underlies our fears of the unknown and of novelties. Those who resist being anaesthetised by ideologies are better off abiding by the paradoxes of psychic life and being energised by the questions they ask. Messages derived from "oracles" can be extremely dramatic, but why buy into the drama? Do we have to consult them, or take them so seriously?

To avoid oracular messages, we might think that we actually read an oracle just as we would "read" one of the Rorschach tables. Instead, we take them as real pictures with real voices and, thus, perpetuate our benumbed condition. We have repeatedly observed this in our recent history. Symington remarks that, "The embodiment of the 'thoughts of a god' has been substituted for thinking" (Symington, 2004, p. 15). Feuds and schisms (also within our psychoanalytic culture) can be seen as indicators of this pervasive human weakness: submission to idols for anaesthetic purposes. People fail to be themselves because it is easier to be somebody else. We can more easily imitate someone else's success than risk our own failure or, paradoxically, risk our own success. In fact, risk can also be unbearable. We are frequently in a hurry to exalt ourselves by imitating what is most successful, and are too paralysed or benumbed to cope with our own thoughts. In the academies, we even call this "disciplinary integrity".

What, essentially, is an ideology? Even though we might not have an exhaustive definition of it, we appreciate the pragmatic/psychoanalytic wisdom that counsels the acceptance of a challenge even in the absence of exact defining terms. An ideology seems to promise that obnoxious forces, oppressive institutions, injustice, and misery can be irrevocably swept away from our existence by means of an innovative world view. Such dramatic social changes, moreover, are believed to unlock our human potential and radically resolve the passivity that is everywhere. For our present purposes, we are not concerned with the visible advancements of innovative ideologies, but with their oversights and blind spots. Through a system of beliefs, our human adversities are all encompassed in a design to combat immemorial injustices, so no distinction is made between different kinds of suffering. From an ideological perspective, different kinds of misery are all regarded as a uniform kind of negative, futile, alienating condition. Examples of the resolution of conflict through regression include the tendency to give up one's individuality by becoming an undifferentiated member of a group. Such a condition is attained through the adhesion to primitive paradigms that are all the more powerful for promising release from tensions and conflicts. Once we are absorbed into a regressive gestalt, there is no more need for effort to mediate between diverse inclinations and prospects. It may be generally conceded that all addictions have the same function of offering comfort in spite of their obvious constrictive nature. Pain comes to be regarded as a purposeless affliction to be eradicated by the exercise of our liberated, revolutionary, ideological rationality. Because they somehow promise the elimination of inner pain, we wholeheartedly espouse ideologies, and accept their rigid conditions for aligning ourselves with their world view. No price is too high for securing the promise of the resolution of inner conflict and general distress. Our recent history gives evidence of the analgesic effects of any world view, and of the high price paid in a single century: about one hundred million casualties.

Involvement in an encompassing ideology is often the false solution to the compulsive use of ever-new tricks and toys, drugs and actions. In Lewis's view, in fact, we are meandering along the path of life in a contentedly shallow condition, absorbed in transactions with friends, or a piece of work that tickles our vanity, a holiday, or a promising new book, when suddenly a stab of pain brings this house of cards tumbling down (Lewis, 2012, p. 106). At first, we are overwhelmed, and all our little analgesics look like broken toys. Then, slowly and reluctantly, little by little, we try to bring ourselves into the frame of mind that we should be in at all times. We remind ourselves that all these distracting toys were never intended to possess our hearts, but the moment the threat is withdrawn, our whole nature leaps back to the toys. It is at this point that a powerful ideology could "rescue" us. "Anyone who does not see the vanity of the world is very vain himself", says Pascal. "So who does not see it, apart from young people whose lives are all noise, diversions, and thoughts for the future?" (Pascal, 1995, p. 3). Take away their diversions and you will see them bored to tears. In Pascal's view, they then fear their nullity, without recognising it, for nothing could be more wretched than to be intolerably depressed as soon as one is reduced to introspection with no means of diversion (Pascal, 1995, p. 3). What would be a "solution of genius"? No more insignificant, limited, temporary treatment for our pangs of anguish. Ultimately, we need a powerful, all-embracing, salvational, transformative world view that we can regard as the encompassing "truth"—and we must belong to it. Adhering to it wholeheartedly then seems to be *the* definitive, permanent solution. The effects of waiting for a social revolution/salvation can truly become the opium of the people, in the sense that opium is an antidote for intolerable pain. However, it can also be a source of drowsiness that hinders proactive actions and inclines only to passive reactions. It is, therefore, futile to believe any of those promises implying that if only some drastic reforms in our system were made, a heaven on earth would follow.

A subjacent belief in contemporary society is that to be anaesthetised to our suffering is an acceptable way to manage it. Nevertheless, this belief overlooks the fact that when we mitigate our discomfort, we do nothing to resolve our complex predicament. Perhaps it is good to explore the irrational faith that we place in emotional anaesthetics. Davies thinks of an irrational faith largely because when our psychic suffering is anaesthetised, it does not simply disappear, but, rather, it is displaced, exported, transmitted. It can be transmitted either to our future selves (in a subsequent phase of life) or to other people. In this sense, then, anaesthetics do not remove suffering. They simply move it from one place/person to another (Davies, 2012, p. 36).

Another accepted way to manage suffering seems related to our natural desire for something greater than ourselves, and this is so strong that it is very difficult to eradicate. Ministering to this need can be a powerful, instant analgesic. Thus, we seek and easily find this psychic something-greater-than-ourselves even in someone we approach for cure, healing, and resolving inner pain. One of the good results of therapy is a capacity to elaborate and abandon these compensatory strategies. Yet, we never really abandon our treasure hunts for the ultimate medicament. Instead, we transform the nature of the healing treasure we are after. To resolve pain in a definitive way, we seek objects/objectives that we believe have some "cosmic value" and, thus, we will do anything to acquire them. Our young, combative heroes are often perceived as the providers, but this is a delusional outlook. In our literary traditions, there are often young heroes presented as the winners and conquerors, and old heroes frequently are described as capable of inner victories, endurance of disaster, and personal transformation. Perhaps we could entirely rethink, or reword, this distinction, and suggest that our heroes are really neither young nor old. Who is old or who is young really? Our heroes could instead be seen as childish/infantile when they risk their lives to acquire something desired and of great relevance to resolving pain. When our heroes are not quite old but are, in fact, mature, then they seek the development of the capacity to cope with the endless struggles of life without succumbing to analgesic remedies. In other words, the young heroes of our intellectual heritage are not simply young; they are sadly infantile and irremediably childish. It is not, ultimately, a question of age, but, rather, of inclining to childish/infantile outlooks or to adult/mature ones.

From a psychoanalytic perspective, the point is that discontent could arise whether the subject attains a goal or does not attain it. The price for these disillusionments is further psychic discontent. Let us not forget that people with enough inner strength to seek therapy often come with the burning desire for a specific something that will resolve all their painful problems. They might desperately want a marriage or a divorce, to lose or gain weight; they might even seek a "magic" fruit from a very special tree or some psychological promised land. The underlying conviction is basically the same: there is something immensely desirable out there and you must get it at any price.

This something can also be an ideal, or collective way of life. Such massive pain-relieving power must be highly rationalised and theorised, but humans are masters at creating social follies. In fact, when there is a will to idealise, or condemn, the ways can be easily found (Chang, 1991, p. 270). The ultimate price for any ideological, salvational venture is the obligation to lie to oneself *and* to others. Whether we think of national socialism, Bolshevism or Maoism, the price for the purported elimination of suffering is an increasing disregard for truth. In Chang's view, there was a time during Maoism when telling fantasies to oneself as well as to others, and believing them, was practised to an incredible degree. Peasants could move crops from several plots of land to a single plot to show officials a miracle harvest. Similar wonderful harvests could be shown off to agricultural "scientists" or visitors who were not informed, or did not want to know. A large part of the population could be swept into a confused, crazy world. Self-deception while deceiving others may influence the entire range of interactions. Those who fail to match other people's fantastic claims begin to doubt and blame themselves. As information is withheld or fabricated, it is very difficult for people to have confidence in their own experience or knowledge (Chang, 1991, p. 270)—not to mention that ideology-dependent people might be facing a tidal wave of fervour that tends to swamp individual cool-headedness. It is then easy to ignore reality and simply put one's faith in a further "–ism", whatever the name. It is always some special something that purports to relieve us from the burden of life. According to Chang, to go along with the collective frenzy is by far the easiest course. To pause and think, and be circumspect, means trouble. Those who do voice doubts are immediately silenced, which also means discrimination against their families and a bleak prospect for their children. This is the general psychological paradigm at different scales of magnitude and intensity, all the way down to a one-to-one perverse organisation. Those who do not believe ridiculous boasting just blindly accept it for fear of being objects of accusation. The totalitarian system in which they are immersed can sap and warp their sense of responsibility. The whole micro- or macro-culture might slide into double-speak. Words become divorced from reality, responsibility, and people's real thoughts. Lies are told with ease because words lose their meanings and cease to be taken seriously by others. In Chang's work, we read:

> Like many others, I was incapable of rational thinking in those days. We were so cowed and contorted by fear and indoctrination that to deviate from the path laid down . . . would have been inconceivable. Besides, we had been overwhelmed by deceptive rhetoric, disinformation, and hypocrisy, which made it virtually impossible to see through the situation and to form an intelligent judgement. (Chang, 1991, p. 378)

Of course, this sort of environment is likely to prove unbearable. We can understand pathology, but we cannot go along with its glorification, still less its right to rule. At this point, we should also say that it can be disquieting to think that a comparable situation could even prevail in other societal constructions, or even in bi-personal contexts. At the same time, it would not be realistic to presume that there can be human enclaves that are totally immune to pathology or deterioration. Just think of the one hundred million casualties of the twentieth century's anaesthetising ideologies; how does that work for the relief of psychic pain?

For the highly intelligent creatures that we are, life would be too painful without some encompassing view of the world conferring sufficient meaning to our itinerary and absorbing most of our emotions. This pervasive, ubiquitous necessity is met through identification with any well-structured conglomeration of beliefs, which we call ideologies for lack of a better term. This necessity is so imperious and unrenounceable that we surrender our entire lives to any promise of meaning. Whether we read Frankl or Solzhenitsyn, we are moved with compassion for the victims of whatever ideology is being examined. However, we tend to forget the repugnant tragedy of the perpetrators who degrade themselves by carrying out the worst atrocities for the sake of their total enslavement to their delusional beliefs in a meliorist, collective promise. Providing examples seems superfluous: we are flooded with them. When competing ideologies are at work one against the other, we could think in terms of deadened subjects trying to defeat other deadened beings.

Along with the well-known explanations in terms of schizo-paranoid behaviour in our cohesive factions, we could seek an enlightening psychoanalytic rendition of the problem by invoking Grotstein's work. He says, "The activity of the 'super' ego *attacks* the subject's *links* with good, helpful objects, thereby preventing him from internalizing the good objects for mental growth and impeding his capacity to learn from experience (think)" (Grotstein, 2009, p. 67). Furthermore, "In the case of "the infant who is fated to become psychotic" the "'super' ego develops before the ego, and when the ego does emerge, it is tyrannized by the 'super' ego" (Grotstein, 2009, p. 67). This condition certainly appears to be a very primitive, rigid, and painful method of survival. Then again, an ideology can be frequently felt as a power even mightier and more aggressive than the primitive ego-tyrannised-by-the-superego conjunction. Total adherence to an ideology can be the only way to actually *storm* this inner structure and finally prevail over the condition. When the fragile ego is tyrannised by the superego, argues Grotstein,

> The patient is, by default, compelled to mobilize his *death instinct* to attack his remaining contact with objects because of the pain of their being tantalizing reminders of necessary and desirable objects that he cannot internalize or metabolise. (Grotstein, 2009, p. 67)

These objects—persons who can be identified with and internalised for purposes of growth—are no longer available in this default, that is, the tyranny of the ego by the superego. The ego would like to mobilise a good, useful object, but, in such a tyrannised condition, it simply cannot succeed. In the case of the infant who is fated to become not quite a psychotic, but a victim of ideology, this mobilising service is provided by any sufficiently powerful worldly faith, in the sense that by dehumanising subjects collectively (how could they do that?

we keep asking), it instigates death instincts in the guise of purity and fidelity, advancement and emancipation; these can eliminate whatever tantalising and (potentially) good objects that they cannot use. No wonder that major (or minor) ideologies are so powerful, and that no price is too high to gain admission to them.

CHAPTER THREE

Psychic "justice"

A concern for psychic "justice"

If we could envisage a post-poverty society, we could still reasonably ask who the poor are among us. We could perhaps say that the psychically poor are those who do not have the inner resources, or capacities, to grow and mature. It would also seem unjust that some of us can be so very poor. We now commonly say that it violates our sense of justice that some of us spend their entire life in absolute poverty—in the sense of insufficient food or shelter. But, what about those who do not have sufficient psychic resources, those who psychically barely survive? Perhaps it is now time to be free enough to consider those who are not resourceful enough to endure the pain that is necessary for maturation and growth. Just as the materially poor feel entitled to some support irrespective of their ability to earn, the generically immature are perhaps entitled to comparable compassionate, supportive treatment. Traditionally, the question of fellow humans who were "starving" was perhaps hardly considered, while recently we think that it is a serious problem. Similarly, the question of insufficient maturational potential could become a legitimate concern. Thus, the question of social psychic justice is either complete nonsense and logically absurd, or else it is worthy of much more attention. In Sen's book, *The Idea of Justice*, we read that a sense of injustice may generate the sort of psychic discontent that could serve as a signal that moves us (Sen, 2009, p. viii). A signal demands critical examination, and there has to be some scrutiny of the soundness of a conclusion based mainly on signals of pain; not all of us can be sufficiently critical to do just that in the course of our development. What is invoked here, however, is an idea of psychic justice in a very personal sense. Its aim is to clarify how *we* can proceed to address questions of enhancing psychic equity and the wish to pursue one's destiny, rather than to offer resolutions about the question of "perfect" justice, of justice *qua* justice. The crucial question remains: why can you pursue your personal destiny while I can only follow an inertial fate? Perhaps social action for those who are homeless, or exploited, will become a thing of the past one day; questions of destiny will remain, however.

With the increasing acceleration of transformations in our culture, we might be fighting one day for the rights of those who are *psychically* poor: envious, omnipotent, rabid, obsessed, etc. Perhaps we will "soon" resolve the problem of inequality of opportunities (to live) on account of unequal food, health, or education. But when it comes to psychic poverty, there will be even more serious combat. It is implausible, of course, to believe that equal opportunities will also solve issues of psychological inequality. When equal opportunities are sufficiently established, there still will be problems of inner inequality. For instance, even where there is extreme poverty for all, some of us are more psychically rich than others. Why? And also, is it right? Think of slaves on a cotton plantation in our recent history, or of slaves in a marble quarry during the Roman empire: some were more gentle, creative, and genial than others. This is the injustice that concerns us here. Why? Because it is puzzling to admire our tiny islands of pure psychoanalytic gold in a sea of benumbment and lack of empathy. The question will no longer be why are some so rich while I am so poor? The question could become why are some so calm, while I am so aggrieved? Even the irate or the immature should claim a right to adequate psychological nourishment.

If we regard biblical scriptures as expressions of the social psychology of the west, we could perhaps regard the seven deadly sins as a treatise of general psycho-pathology. The rights that we should promote are those of the people still in the grip of deadening forces. Our emancipatory concerns should no longer be limited to widows, orphans, or minorities. We should seek to promote justice for narcissists, obsessives, paranoids, and other fellow sufferers. Physical assistance might have to be transformed into psychological support. Any constructive move in the area of human suffering implies some degree of tolerance of psychic pain. There is, therefore, a systemic injustice in the distribution of our capacity to endure pain. Those who are not strong enough to endure a minimal level of psychic pain are virtually reduced to a stagnant condition. They are those who simply cannot sustain the burden of life and, thus, cannot truly live it. Not only do they automatically place the burden on others and are sometimes ruthlessly rejected; when pain is unbearable, they automatically resort to compensatory strategies that ultimately make life even more difficult. In our society, we tend to avoid homelessness even for those who are incapable of obtaining some abode. Similarly, we could learn to assume some responsibility for those who do not succeed in winning for themselves an indispensable minimal capacity to endure frustration. By way of professional distortion, psychoanalysts tend always to see psychic forces at work. In this sense, the poorest of the poor, the lowest of the lowly are those who remain excluded from maturation and creativity because they do not have the strength to face the necessary pain and are, thus, forced to resort to somatisation, symptomatic anaesthetics, mindlessness, etc. In a very rough and general sense, are not these subjects most in need of our compassion? Conservatives are inclined to say of the materially poor that they do not try hard enough, that they are lazy and want to be fed by others, but even in our tough meritocratic world, we believe that those who do not work are entitled to sufficient food and shelter. The same is true for those who are deficient in their capacity to tolerate pain and, thus, cannot engage in the innumerable processes of working through, elaboration, and re-creation of their personal experiences. The poorest of the poor—from a psychological perspective—might become our primary objects of compassionate empathy. We are told by different psychoanalytic authors that the capacity for creative suffering is the key to the fulfilment of our destiny. Is it fair that some of us do not have the resources to attempt just this, one might ask. As if we were saying, "Why don't you mature?", and as if we were answered, "Because it is too painful for me even to try."

We could conceive of destiny as a limited yet meaningful context of freedom; destiny is, thus, understood as integral to the self rather than the result of external gravitational forces. Consequently, destiny cannot be reduced to the category of causality, or derived from total freedom—whatever that might be. Destiny is indeed bound to freedom—which is rather limited. Since destiny is linked with our limited freedom, it might also involve inherent contradictions. The fact of contradiction points to the essential distinction between fate and destiny. The idea of destiny embraces a wide range of free or fated possibilities and is not a question of a simple process explicable in linear terms. In fact, destiny combines both the choice aspect and the determination aspect; in contrast, fate excludes any sense of choice.

The belief that people have a right to complain and that they should not suffer injustice in silence is implicit in all movements for social emancipation. However, individually, this right is also implicit in the desire for personal psychic health and maturity. Why be left to an inertial fate when we could pursue our destiny? Thus, from my perspective, fate might come to appear as the default of destiny. Perhaps our legitimate complaints will "soon" be about *psychic* equity rather than *material* equity. It is interesting to invoke at this point the theses of Frankl and Solzhenitsyn. In *Man's Search for Meaning*, Frankl vividly demonstrates that inner psychic force at times enables the less hardy camp/war prisoners to survive the experience better than those who are physically stronger (Frankl, 2007). In *The Gulag Archipelago*, Solzhenitsyn (1974) develops a similar theory and comes to the same conclusion. Paradoxically, these subjects are the rich of this world; and we could regard it as an injustice that some of us may be psychically less robust. Ultimate justice and social equity should be directed to help the psychically poor. The idea of justice might be transferred from the tangible domain onto the psychological level. In Pascal's view, "Justice is a point so fine that our instruments are too blunt to touch it exactly" (Pascal, 1995, p. 9). This observation is all the more true for psychic justice—if we can envision it at all.

The underlying question remains as to whether or not it is fair that one is capable of internalising whatever source of benevolence there is, using it for growth and freedom, while another is just not capable of internalising any kind of (limited) love, and settles instead for sheer hatred and schizoid attitudes. This question is probably legitimate, or else it does not make sense at all. This problem seems to resonate intensely with our contemporary culture in the sense that it is frequently expressed in the myths of our popular literature: for instance, in the acclaimed *Harry Potter* saga, He Who Must Not Be Named had a suicidal mother and a deserting father, while *our* Harry Potter had a heroic mother who freely gave her life to save her child. His father would probably qualify as a "good enough" parent by Winnicottian standards. But then, this looks like an unfair share in parental love, or else an unfair share in the innate capacity to use whatever love we can have. Notwithstanding the hateful foster parents, Harry becomes a sure winner, forever fooling and escaping You Know Who, the obsessive destroyer. The critical difference lies in Harry's psychic energy, which is probably due to the sort of love, however quantitatively minimal, that he was able to absorb. Indeed, who cares about a vindictive policy if one has inner courage and sufficient self-esteem? What about those who do not: the creeps, the envious, the vicious, the perverse? A homogenisation of such features can possibly create the astute killer who craves immortality and who ultimately destroys himself. It is, indeed, a fertile topic for reflection. If the function of personal response comes to be theoretically excluded, one might be restricted by a very tight mechanism of cause and effect that renders one prone to perverse entitlement. If one is "ontologically" entitled to having caring parents and this has not been the case, then one seems to have the right to a non-negotiable compensation in terms of interpersonal strategies. If the compensation is not forthcoming, it is actually a perverse "ethical" duty to exercise all of one's considerable cunning to extort what is needed—horcruxes and all that. The best way to make sure that one is given love and respect is to coerce others to give as much love and respect as is needed. To this effect, one should expediently control the minds of the others by inhabiting them and attuning their minds to one's own. This is done by inducing a mental numbing of the other that facilitates control, that makes him feed on one's own epistemology, that turns him into an "eater" of a perverse logic—simply that.

We could ask an unavoidable question: which are the injustices we should cope with, once the material injustices are removed?

> What moves us, reasonably enough, is not the realization that the world falls short of being completely just—which few of us expect—but that there are clearly remediable injustices around us which we want to eliminate. (Sen, 2009, p. vii)

This sense of injustice is evident enough in our everyday life with all the iniquity and subjugation that we may suffer and resent, but it also applies to more widespread instances of injustice pertaining to our intangible psychic life. In Sen's view, understanding inescapably involves reasoning. We have to "read" what we feel and seem to see, and ask what these perceptions indicate and how we may take them into account without being overwhelmed by them (Sen, 2009, p. vi).

Throughout psychoanalytic culture, it is iterated that the capacity to endure some frustration is the key to growth and maturity. Paradoxically, the capacity to accept, to acknowledge, psychic injustice becomes the prerequisite for remedying it constructively. Think of courage, for instance: we all would like more of it. Even experts often see it as a kind of mythic power, existing only in "heroes" who are beyond human fear; courage is now a fertile field of concern for human psychology. The really rich are those who have it, those who can endure pain on their way to growth. More precisely, courage is ultimately the ability to act in the presence of fear, not without it. Courage is the capacity to endure the difficult companion that is fear. We should learn to focus on how fear feels at any given moment. Paradoxically, it is only when fear itself no longer scares us that we can be proactive in its presence. This is perhaps what courage is. When we can manage this, we can be truly rich. When we cannot manage it, we are psychically poor—and thus most deserving of compassion and support. This is ultimately social justice at the psychic level. In fact, the opportunity of meeting someone new and different often appears too frightening and, thus, we might even opt for endogamy or isolation. The people who get the most opportunities to create friendships and to develop love relationships are not simply those who appear as the best. They are those who are capable of risking contact and of not remaining frozen in the warmth of infantile relations, those who can endure a modicum of pain and, thus, grow. The lives of narcissists might then appear rather limited. Is it fair that some of us can mature more than others? When adversity comes, the more mature ones almost welcome it, knowing that it will deepen their relationship with higher psychic dimensions. Their reward is the ever-present support of inner creativity. This gives them reasonable confidence—they are the rich, then.

In Davies' view, the "being mode" advocated by Fromm has, as its prerequisites, a sufficient level of independence *and* the presence of critical reason. "Its fundamental characteristic is that of being active, not in the sense of outward activity, of busyness, but of *inner* activity. To be active is to give expression to one's faculties and talents" (Davies, 2012, p. 105). In this way, we may ultimately transcend our managerial, limited ego. Again, those who opt for being are the truly rich ones. Compassion and social support should be especially reserved for those who are deficient in the being mode. This is, perhaps, an unfamiliar perspective, but it is clinically essential and could become socially urgent. It is commonly believed that the having mode is not essential to human nature, and that it is induced by social conditions shaped by a consumerist, competitive society. The problematic point is that in this way we have found some causal, external factor, indeed a "culprit", and we may, thus, slide into a paranoid outlook on human life. As is known, the having mode of life directs our energy towards pursuing a lifestyle that diminishes our capacity to *be*, by making the acquisition of goods and social positions more important than the attainment of psychic growth. However, those who cannot *be* are those who cannot endure the psychic pain of entering the dimension of being. Ultimately, the true poor who need help are those who cannot enter creative suffering. From the being vertex of observation, people are wealthy not because they *have* a great deal but because they *are* great. They measure their wealth not in terms of their material possessions, but in terms of how far they have developed their human potential to think and work creatively (Davies, 2012, p. 105). Is this fair? Ultimately, perhaps, we would all like *to be* rather than *to have*. Thus, differences of degree in the domain of being could frame new questions in the outlook of an ulterior dimension of justice.

Fate as the default of destiny

We would probably gladly renounce any form of triumphal collective fate for the sake of a personal destiny, however laborious and limited. As is known, the nature of the lives that people can lead has been the object of attention of social psychologists over the years. In Sen's view, the much-used economic criteria of advancement reflected in readily produced statistics have tended to focus specifically on the inanimate objects of convenience, while we are more interested in what these objects can do to the human lives that they can directly or indirectly influence (Sen, 2009, p. 233). The case for using, instead, direct indicators of the quality of life and of inner wellbeing is now increasingly recognised. One of these indicators is the reasonable personal conviction of trying to fulfil one's own destiny. One's destiny tends to be personal and hard won; it has to be contrasted with the general notion of fate, which seems to involve only psychic passivity. In Freud's words, "As for the great necessities of Fate, against which there is no help, they [we] will learn to endure them with resignation" (Freud, 1927c, p. 50)—with passivity, indeed. In Sen's outlook, the "capabilities approach" focuses on *personal* life (in contrast to collective fate), and not just on any detached objects of convenience that a person may possess and which are often taken to be the main criteria of human success (Sen, 2009, p. 233), thus, ultimately, some sort of pseudo-destiny. In fact, the "capabilities approach" proposes a serious departure from the means of living towards the actual opportunities of living (Sen, 2009, p. 269). This also helps to bring about a change of perspective that detaches us from means-orientated evaluative approaches, which are all-purpose means such as wealth and power: detachment from this means-orientated outlook and attachment to what? To the pursuit of whatever is our meaningful personal destiny. In fact, the "capabilities approach" is pre-emptively concerned with correcting the focus on means and directing it on the opportunity to fulfil one's life, to attain sufficient freedom, and to achieve one's reasoned ends. This is, ultimately, a focus on one's destiny, as contrasted to fate. In this outlook, of course, we cannot settle for the mere avoidance of psychic distress. In Freud's terms, we cannot be "content to aim at an avoidance of unpleasure—a goal, as we might call it, of weary resignation" (Freud, 1930a, p. 82).

Kierkegaard happens to suggest that a personal destiny is possible, however poor we are: "We shall, with the powers we have, seek to make this as enlightening as possible, to bring as close as possible to the poor the consolation he has in being able to be merciful" (Kierkegaard, 1962, p. 293). Even just being able to be merciful, when nothing else is possible, is an escape from an impersonal fate in which we are inert. We can fulfil a personal destiny, rather than being ensnared in a collective fate, even if that is one of maximal affluence. Being merciful? Only that? We could not possibly say "only that" after coming so very close to being swept into disparate, disastrous, triumphal fates. However, even fulfilling a "modest" personal destiny, rather than collapsing inert into fate, can be a privilege worthy of the utmost attention. At the intersection of fate and destiny we have the intense inner experience to which we may point with words such as choice, decision, and obstinacy. The intersection of fate and choice brings us back to the developmental task: we may complain, but it is ours to do. In fact, the idea of a personal destiny is so complex and enigmatic that it might even include failure.

For example, let us consider the modern-day story of Liz Murray, as reported by Hood in *The Self Illusion* (Hood, 2011, p. viii). This is not a story of failure, but of great success: by the time Liz was fifteen years old, her mother had died of AIDS and her HIV-infected father had moved into care. She found herself homeless and looking after her younger sister. In spite of all these obstacles, she excelled in school and won a scholarship to Harvard University, eventually graduating in 2009. Her "Homeless to Harvard" tale can be an inspiring account of the triumph of the individual self over adversity. It is, perhaps, the epitome of what was called the "American Dream"—and the reason why so many love her story. But let us pause for a moment and think again. What is the gist of the message? Is it that if we try hard enough we can all achieve our dreams? Clearly, this cannot be true. "Homeless to Harvard" is more a tale about the psychic inequalities that exist in our lives. Liz Murray is remarkable, but this means that she is also the exception rather than the rule, because most individuals never overcome the hurdles that keep them from success. Most people could not endure the pain of such adversities—and a comparable story could even end tragically (Hood, 2011, p. 14). In this case, the determining circumstances are certainly not social, but psychological: she was able to cope with suffering. The question surfaces: are we really responsible for this capacity? It is a condition, perhaps, comparable to being exceptionally brilliant or beautiful. Such a story certainly engages our evolving idea of justice, indeed of psychic justice.

As I have said, the idea of a personal destiny could include failure. Many of us might consider Liz Murray to be one of life's winners, but the other side of the coin is that we all too easily regard those who fail as losers. Our view of the game of life might become so distorted that we primarily (or exclusively) blame individuals rather than the circumstances that prevent them from achievement. On the other hand, it can also be misleading to primarily (or exclusively) blame circumstances. It almost feels as if we were arbitrarily shifting from one outlook to another. This is known as the common attribution error in human reason: when *other* people fail it is because they are psychically inadequate—or, simply, losers. When *I* fail it is because of my adverse circumstances (Hood, 2011, p. 14). This is something worth knowing and watching out for. What we advocate here is a more balanced and psychologically fertile approach. Outward and inner determinants are, of course, both at work. Nevertheless, we could reasonably suggest that inner resources for psychic growth and achievement are more often vulnerable to obscurity, and this is why we try assiduously to explore the question of our relative tolerance of psychic pain. Kierkegard again: "Suffering terrible inner torment I became a writer", that is, he fulfilled his destiny rather than being shaped by impersonal fate: "Truly something not automatically granted to many in each generation" (Kierkegaard, 1996, p. 541).

We can then ask, with Hollis, how we could argue that we are free to pursue our destiny, or live *our own* journey, when we are, in fact, constrained by that most transient of realities—the fevers and fashions of our popular culture (Hollis, 2003, p. 33). Perhaps contemporary illnesses are being overcome by a collective fate, in the form of a very positive and affluent one. Winnicott, instead, would regard illness as the inhibition of that potential spontaneity that, for him, characterises creative living (Corradi Fiumara, 2009). The complex vicissitudes of identification that appear in Zweig's story—reported in "Dostoevski and parricide"—invite Freud to conclude that even if the protagonist escaped unconscious transference, "fate was able to catch her at an undefended spot" (Freud, 1928b, pp. 193–194). Perhaps we must work relentlessly for our destiny if we do not want to be caught by an inertial Fate at undefended passages. It takes integrity to navigate through the meanderings of our identifications if we try to pursue our destiny and escape fate.

Browsing through Jung's comments on the practice of psychotherapy, we read:

> About a third of my cases are not suffering from any clinically definable neurosis, but from the senselessness and aimlessness of their lives. I should not object if this were called the general neurosis of our age. Fully two thirds of my patients are in the second half of life. (Jung, quoted in Storr, 1997, p. 193)

This probably indicates that they are somehow concerned with their own destiny. If we fail to pursue our own journey, we might remain immobilised in the general mechanics of fate. This is perhaps our new fight for emancipatory justice. If we are not engaged in this struggle, we might easily forget our present moment. In Pascal's *Human Happiness*, he instructively remarks that

> We never keep to the present. We recall the past; we anticipate the future as if we found it too slow in coming and were trying to hurry it up, or we recall the past as if to stay its too rapid flight. We are so unwise that we wander about in times that do not belong to us, and do not think of the only one that does; so vain that we dream of times that are not and blindly flee the only one that does. *The fact is that the present usually hurts*. (Pascal, 1995, p. 10; my emphasis)

Here, again, the lucky ones are those who can endure the hurt. In different traditions there are innumerable ways of *training* our young to *endure small frustrations*; it is actually a coaching for going through some bearable difficulties in order to reach maturity. These customs, of course, are generally ridiculed by our enlightened epistemologies, which tend to include these educational efforts in the domain of mere subjugation, oppression, sadism, and filicide. Needless to say, this is a sophisticated, perverse way of using one piece of truth in order to avoid seeing more truth. In fact, we can be cheated by both falsity and truth, and so it is our excessive vulnerability that causes us to escape the present moment and take refuge in past and future. The "here and now" principle of interpretative action in psychoanalysis (as opposed to reaction) teaches us just that. Yet, the only occasion for creatively dealing with our personal destiny is the current moment we live. And the problem is twofold. The escape from the present is not only due to vulnerability to a painful present. The "invulnerable" individuals may also become deprived of a sense of destiny because they pass unscathed through a present that does not touch them with distress. If we let ourselves escape from our present moment, we impede the possibility of pursuing a destiny. Our inclination to adhere to the so-called non-existent past and non-existent future can imprison us in the gravitational mechanics of fate. This lapse into passivity yields the sort of imitative complaints that inhibit our pursuit of a personal journey. How is it that something as important as complaint can, in another guise, be so pointless? At its worst, complaint can be a useless waste of energy, a futile cry against the inevitable, a refusal to accept reality for what it is. According to Baggini, "To answer this question we would need to understand the myriad ways in which complaining can be abused and misused" (Baggini, 2010, p. 19) in an impersonal, unreasoned way.

The unduly scared person, that is, the person who is not in search of his unique destiny, can be forced paradoxically to make the choices that will not contribute to his inner flourishing. In our current culture of so-called "lay rationalism" there is a tendency to base decisions on rationalistic, *hard* attributes, such as economic values, rather than *soft* attributes, such as the inclination to creativity (Haybron, 2010, pp. 234–235). Roughly, the idea is that we often choose options that are far better according to hard criteria like monetary or social payoff, even when we can predict that these options will be detrimental to our psychic experience of life. The potential of our current rationalism to impede psychic fulfilment should not be underestimated: probably the most important features of life, beyond the bare necessities of existence, tend to be intangible or "soft", and, hence, at a disadvantage when compared to "harder", visible factors. The less lucky, the poor, thus feel forced to choose by hard logic, egoic criteria, rather than by the forces of one's deeper self—the "I" of the personality. They cannot afford the risk of getting into trouble and must, therefore, exclusively abide by hard logic, which can be contrary to the challenge of a personal destiny. We need the present moment to shape a destiny instead of lapsing into some mechanical, inertial fate. In a popular saga of our times, the young Harry Potter, in a gradual, inconspicuous way—in the course of several volumes—manages to bring his best friend to really play, to "play" in the fullest sense, not just Quidditch. In fact, not being able to play is a psychic drama, a total injustice, but something that can be remedied, it seems. The hero's friend becomes free to use his present moments, finally detached from whoever is there to push him into the past, or into the future. He is, thus, helped to fulfil his destiny. Pascal writes, "Let each of us examine his thoughts; he will find them wholly concerned with the past or the future"—as analysts know so well. "Thus we never actually live, but hope to live, and since we are always planning how to be happy, it is inevitable that we should never be so" (Pascal, 1995, p. 10). It seems unfair that we cannot manage to use our now. The question is how we can resolve this injustice and make use of that priceless resource that we call "present", potentially available to each one of us. Indeed, how can we possibly play in the past or in the future? No matter what the cost can be, we need to be encouraged to steer towards a personal destiny rather than impersonal, collective fate. There is often a feeling of some ultimate inexplicable rage, as if we felt that we are robbed of something and that we are just going along with some inertial fate—even though it might be a very "good" one.

In Haybron's view, the essential question could be, is human psychology well adapted to managing high levels of option freedom? A liberal, rationalistic view claims just that. Roughly, given the greatest possible option of freedom, and otherwise reasonably favourable conditions, individuals will tend to choose prudently, so that most can expect to do well in the course of their lives, and better than they would if given less freedom to shape their lives (Haybron, 2010, p. 229). But will they fulfil their destiny? Perhaps this liberal, optimistic, meliorist, comforting outlook cannot honestly be maintained: in fact, it is all too often falsified. According to Ferro, we should recall that symptoms, or defences, are the result of years of hard work to avoid *worse* trouble, and so, in Ferro's view, deconstructing and constructing are processes that *"given the threshold of tolerance to pain* require care and vigilance" (Ferro, 2011, p. 37; my emphasis). In fact, constructing and deconstructing are essential to our maturational journey. Suppose we solved the world problems of food and shelter for all: we would still remain with most of our psychic problems. Suppose, as Ferro iterates, that psychic reality and outer reality were equally real, and suppose there is a major shift from the pre-eminence of outer reality to the pre-eminence of psychic reality (Ferro, 2011, p. 37). We would still face a problem of poverty. In fact, if the capacity that makes the difference in therapeutic and maturational ventures is the "given threshold of tolerance to pain", an entirely new picture would emerge for us: the real poor of this world are those who are lacking in the capacity to tolerate pain, those who have very little of it, who can barely mature and even become ill. Ill? It is not only a question of illness: we might be unable to live a personal life. Since we cannot endure inner pain too well, and seek all sorts of anaesthetics, we could say that we are in a period of psychic famine, and that most of our manic defences are a tragic masquerade. "In short", says Ferro,

> I believe that when the mind is able to produce alpha elements we are already in a state of 'abundance' (of *fat kine*—cows); ... Today's "famine" (*lean kine*) corresponds to situations where there is a hypofunction or alpha "α-function (a defective or missing alpha function).
> (Ferro, 2011, p. 88)

We must, therefore, enrich our *nourishing* resources. We should make a constant effort to generate joint "myths" in the consulting room: they can function as narratable precipitates of experience and can open for us ever-new perspectives.

Some analysts believe that providing a secure milieu in which the patient can explore and express his most intimate thoughts and feelings is at least as important as any interpretations which they might offer. According to Davies, in a climate that is largely hostile to emotional suffering, anyone who suggests that suffering is integral to our wellbeing may appear eccentric or even masochistic. In his words, "Such an individual may even be summarily dismissed as an unhappy person who simply has a vendetta against the happy life" (Davies, 2012, p. 9). While the happiness movements believe that a happy life is largely reached by denying, avoiding, or anaesthetising psychic pain, the present outlook suggests that human happiness is never easily won. It can be reached for by understanding what our suffering is trying to teach us. Paradoxically, a happy life is not achieved by directly seeking it, or through the drastic avoidance of suffering, but, rather, through our willingness to confront, experience, and learn from our suffering whenever it may arise. In his work on avoiding/living emotions, Ferro provides innumerable clinical illustrations of just this basic attitude.

Our stubborn need to avoid pain might even influence one's choice of occupation; the choice could depend excessively on matters like income, visibility, power, as opposed to how inwardly rewarding it will be. Our generic rationalism could help us to explain the prevalence of so called materialism *without* having to claim that people are overwhelmed by materialistic values. In fact, for the most part, the values that people commonly endorse are decidedly non-materialistic (Haybron, 2010, p. 235). Clearly, there appears to be a massive disconnection between people's values and the way we live. It may simply be that our proclaimed most important values fare poorly in rationalistic terms next to values such as possessions and visible power, which we seek in order to win approval. So, in our generalised splitting attitude, our choices fail to cohere with our values. As is widely believed, some individuals are *fated* to build up an insufficiently coherent personality because of the immaturity of their parents' responses to them in childhood, or because of the absence of empathic parental understanding. As is known, Kohut maintains that the child needs to interact with parents who reinforce the sense of self because they mirror the child's developing identity. What if the parents do not? Why then, do so many creatively survive even under the worst circumstances? In our effort to elucidate a psychoanalytic understanding of the fate/destiny question, we should also point out that inadequate parents too often function as self-willed mirrors; they will reflect only what they wish to see and, thus, force the developing person into a debilitating conflict between how one feels and what one is obliged to see and, consequently, feel. Obliged feelings? We could say that the privileged, gifted ones who can pursue their own destiny are not those who have had a good mother, but those who can actually manage to cope with a coercive one: that is, refuse compulsory feelings. This more focused distinction may certainly help us clinically and socially, but then, how separated are our clinical and social experiences?

From the "social" to the "psychological"

We need to translate into a psychological language the vocabulary that we use in describing our efforts to eliminate tangible injustice. We fight forms of oppression such as slavery or the subjugation of minorities; this could also translate into a combat against forms of psychic enslavement to inner pathological organisations, or suffocation of libidinal aspects of the self. For the sake of illustration, let us consider the desire to be nurturing individuals—even though this desire usually manifests as a minor(ity) voice: in fact, this voice is frequently silenced by the ruling inner and social organisation. At times, we almost feel that this desire should not exist, as if there were something suspect about it. Yet, it does exist, and it can even happen that, for "a fraction of votes", it may temporarily exercise some governance and redirect our psychic gaze (Phillips & Taylor, 2009, pp. 89–92). The inclination to nurture and care is not some ephemeral, wishful, irrelevant current of the self. When this propensity is subjugated, it can be as frustrating as being coerced into the mortification of sexual life. If we think of eros as a most comprehensive term, the desire to nurture can be thought of as one of its many faces—an intense, significant one. The inclination to be caring and responsible can be as powerful as other drives, even though we customarily ignore its frequent subjugation. Perhaps even the "worst" person has been ruthlessly mutilated in this specific yearning of the self. Yet, we have no remorse about stifling our inclination to care. The foreclosure of our desire for caring can be as devastating as the taboos of sexuality. In fact, when sexuality is excluded we feel that there has been a fraud. We want our share of eros, but we cannot be content either without our share of agape, animating our desire for care and nurture, kindness, and custody. We rarely think of the diffuse sense of humiliation about not being capable of caring love. Phillips and Taylor ask why the pleasures of care astonish us. Paradoxically, disclosing the joys of custody and nurture almost appears as an obscure revelation, as if it were usually regarded as some fictitious, compensatory strategy (Phillips & Taylor, 2009, Chapter One). Not only is our propensity for kindness and custody vulnerable to obscurity, but also its foreclosure/exclusion is not even considered as a worthy problem.

When we protest against systematic medical neglect, we might also want to transfer the complaint to our "right" to obtain help in surviving mentally. We need to help and be helped in the productive management of psychic suffering. We commonly fight to repudiate the permissibility of violence, while we are not so prepared to combat forms of psychic offence, which can be as common and as ubiquitous. We fight to reject the quiet tolerance of chronic hunger while we tend to ignore our equally serious condition of psychic hunger. This incipient change of outlook corresponds to an evolution comparable to the transition from a biologic existence to a dialogic mental life. Once women have completely won their battles for equal opportunities, what will they fight for? The forthcoming challenge is perhaps a transition from the social domain to the psychic level, and, thus, to a more vital two-way communication. The question will no longer be, "Why are you so powerful?" but, "Why are you so calm?" No more questions, perhaps, such as, "Why are you paid more than me for equal work?" but, "Why are you so creative in the face of a tribulation which is equal for all of us?"

The impossibility of remaining silent on a given subject is an observation that can be made about many cases of patent injustice; these move us to rage in a way that is hard for our reason to capture. Yet, according to Sen, any analysis of injustice would also demand clear articulation and reasoned scrutiny (Sen, 2009). In the attempt at a closer look, we could suggest that it is truly unfair not to be able, not to be strong enough, to fight back against subjugation and oppression. Similarly, it seems unjust not to have the inner resources that enable us to survive psychically, to fight psychic entropy, and progress in personal development. Of course, we would all like to avoid psychic colonisation by ideologies, stabilised idealisations, anaesthetising addictions, imitative travesties, and the like. We rage about psychic oppression and would like to explore the forces that we could use against any form of immobilising oppression—in fact, colonisation. Thus, perhaps, what we need is a capacity to shift in our perspectives from the outlook of the psyche to the outlook of culture. Perhaps it is now time to freely move in both directions in the range between the social and the psychological emancipatory questions. And we can now consider psychic reality as our communal human habitat. We should remember, in this connection, that we constantly run the risk of believing that interpersonal circumstances are the primary cause of psychic adversity. This attitude would amount to a paranoid starting point which would definitely relieve us from the labours of the so called "depressive position", that is, the endurance of the inner coexistence of good and evil within our own mind. It is true that Laius arranged for Oedipus to be killed. But then, the solution of the problem is not the physical action of eliminating Laius in retaliation, on the tangible, historical level. The truly creative solution stems from a psychic, inner action: the elimination/digestion/metabolisation of the Laius inside Oedipus's mind.

The emancipatory battles that we conduct for social justice should gradually translate into the psychic domain. Problems of subjugation, exploitation, and control can be resolved in the concrete historical domain in the way of precursors of comparable vicissitudes in the mental domain, both personal and interpersonal. Physical hunger is, of course, an urgent problem, just as is the affectual hunger that puts in jeopardy psychic survival. The issue of equal opportunities should probably translate into the legitimate rights of different aspects of our personality (even our potential agape, our desire to be nurturing), and in general of our human psycho-diversity. The incipient right to escape from the enclaves of horror might translate into the escape from psychopathological prisons. It is now a question of a two-way movement from the historical to the psychic, and conversely. The psychoanalytic setting teaches us to use any bit of behaviour to explore corresponding psychic dynamics. Why? Because it is primarily at this level that the problem must be resolved. Likewise, any psychic vicissitudes can translate into tangible historical events. From the point of view of a two-way communication between the psychic and the social domain, we could be free to creatively reverse our questions; we would then ask what are the psychological effects of interpersonal oppression, or solidarity, and which are the historical/social effects of psychic vicissitudes. And ultimately, psychic difficulties are significantly weighing on social costs. The current management of our affective pain probably accounts for the absorption of most of our world resources.

Whether we seek antidotes for our fear of death, or fear of loneliness, for the fear of losing physical territories or epistemic spaces, there is always the immense cost of coping with such troublesome affects, a cost that is still perplexingly ignored. This issue can at least be an indication of the irrefutable need to somehow envisage the social repercussions of our affective pain, a cost which is often concealed in an endless variety of (perverse) mechanisms with which we can hardly cope. If we think of the cost of ethological human conflicts used to anaesthetise pain, the cost of collapses in morale, of paralysing ideological attitudes, we could also begin to speculate on the enormous gains to be derived from a wiser relationship with our psychic suffering. This is, of course, a high-toned question, and yet, in the language of Haraway, "We are in a world of immensurable results, a world that exceeds its representations and blasts syntax" (Haraway, 1996, p. xiv): a world that is perhaps ready for a new culture, more hospitable to these questions. We could, indeed, ask what the cost is of insufficient mathematical intelligence, *and* what is the cost of insufficient affective maturity. Questions like this, which would not make sense in a culture of years past, can now be met with adequate means for organising usable answers. We can now estimate the costs of environmental degradation or deforestation, just as we can evaluate the benefits of biodiversity and sunshine. From this perspective, affective maturity and psychic harmony are not only positive ideals for our culture, but actually social *assets* whose deterioration will, no doubt, cause serious, costly damage. Questions such as what the cost is of the latest earthquake are probably regarded as acceptable and answerable, as are questions regarding the value of a region's reception of sunshine. Similarly, we could now ask legitimate questions regarding the estimate of cost for any identifiable resurgence of chauvinism, revanchism, ethnocentrism—or intolerance of suffering. For instance, we might ask what percentage of a ticket cost is absorbed by security, that is, the management of fear. Perhaps most of it. Yet, there may be a paradox at work here: it derives from the unprecedented conjunction between the factual possibility of posing these sorts of questions and the persistent inner difficulty of facing them. In fact, an insufficient realisation of our psychic vicissitudes might have an enormous cost for the entire human community. We have reached the point of no return in globalisation and in the capacity to assess the costs–benefits of what we feel and do. We can now, perhaps, begin to calculate the costs of wounded self-esteem, of a shattered cultural identity, or mistrust; these costs can amount to appalling expense.

At one time, we used such sloganised terms as "human community" in a somewhat wishful, pious, idealistic sense, while nowadays the term becomes almost mandatory: we are, in fact, increasingly united, not only by the environment that we create, but also, perhaps primarily, by the psychic atmosphere that we generate and absorb. As is known, some countries are more responsible than others for the emission of toxic waste into our atmosphere; there is also a tendency to make them actually pay for the production of such poisonous, non-recyclable substances. Similarly, in the interpersonal domain, some individuals are more polluting than others, and then ultimately we share the costs of dealing with their production of interpersonal toxicity, but they cannot pay. We just need a new, ulterior logic. In this connection, it is worth remembering that the transition from the medical level of psychoanalysis to the complex psychic condition of human life, seems already to have been clearly advocated by Freud; it is sufficiently revealed whenever we do not read him exclusively for clinical purposes. Freud clearly expresses his interest for the essential understanding of our human condition in one of his letters to Pfister. He writes,

> Also I have often said that I hold that the purely medical importance of analysis is outweighed by its importance to science as a whole, and that its general influence by means of clarification and the exposure of error exceeds its therapeutic value to the individual. (Meng & Freud, 1963, p. 119)

By way of "clinical" example, we might even use the remarks of Debora Spar, expressing herself as president of Barnard College of Columbia University (Spar, 2013). Rather than opportunely commenting on some triumphal students' achievement, rather than exhibiting a condescending attitude towards psychic pain, rather than totally adhering to her professional role and to the attached attitude of smile-or-die, Spar allows herself a daring expression such as, "Sometimes I am sad". If a university president admitted of occasionally being a libertine, it would perhaps be less inappropriate than admitting of some times being *sad*. Indeed, a very creative, brave attitude. In an "unscientific" piece of writing titled "Fear of failing", Spar argues that even in sexuality there is an underlying defensive attitude towards pain that can be ultimately deadening. This attitude can smother a sense of adventure, or an embrace of risk that transcends sexuality and which may, in fact, involve our own inner world. In Spar's gaze, even though young adults might have taken dance classes and saxophone lessons, and might throw themselves into ever-increasing activities such as clubs, study groups, political parties, and internships, "Very few, it seems, have time to catch their breath"—much less to embark upon adventures that do not lead to specific ends. She concludes, "Sometimes I am awestruck by their energy and ambition. But sometimes *I am sad*". Perhaps she sometimes feels *sad* because she cannot quite perceive the involvement of one's deeper psychic self, the capacity for romance, psychic intimacy, and risk. "Catching their breath" probably means reconnecting to their "deeper" ("higher", "more central"—it depends on the geometrical metaphor we choose) inner world. This is a psychic dimension where elaboration, processing, and integration are necessary to avoid fragmentation and crisis. If we let our disparate vicissitudes enter our mind and if we can repossess them, we can more consciously accept our "fear of failing"; we are then in a better position to nurture our innovative, creative use of inner pain. The fear-of-failure, *per se*, may only paralyse us, impede the transition to the psychic domain, and justly make president Spar feel "sad". But she allows herself to feel sad sometimes because she is perhaps not so terrified of psychic pain and is capable of using it for a more profound and realistic understanding of the community, niche, habitat, college she lives for.

> Like when an extraordinary young woman broke down in my office, worried that her commitment to an incredible off-campus activity might drag her grade-point average from an A- to a B+ . . . Some of this is natural, since college has always been a busy time of life. (Spar, 2013, p. 7)

But it is also *sad* because there is no transition from the academic to the psychic. Spar, in fact, believes that much of this intense activity is fine and certainly well intentioned, but the fear of falling short, of disappointing others and their own well-laid plans is also bequeathed upon this generation. However, she does not appear intimidated by the potential disapproval of those who might think that she is not defending her role, as if it were a scandal to feel sad sometimes, as if there were some diffuse, stifling hypocrisy. And she proceeds with her sincere remarks; imparting a lesson of professional integrity, she suggests that, perhaps, "Even the custom of hook-ups (. . . anonymous couplings) are being driven by this fear", essentially the fear of psychic pain that comes from failing. Hook-ups can be the logical conclusion of free, relaxing sexuality, with no risk of rejection. Spar summarises her outlook thus: "By taking away the complexities of romance, the adventure of love is removed and with that the heady, terrifying prospect of falling hard and losing control" (Spar, 2013, p. 71).

CHAPTER FOUR

The shadow revisited

Percival and the engineering sanctuary

Seen at a distance, Percival could appear to be some sort of homeless boy or *clochard*; on closer inspection, one could appreciate that he was perfectly clean. His clothes, however, were assembled to cover rather than dress himself. He had curly brown hair and a beard that, together, abundantly covered his head—or perhaps concealed it. What was remarkable was the gentle twinkle in his blue eyes and a meek attitude. He moved and behaved as if he was ashamed of occupying space in my office or of soiling it. But he looked peacefully into my eyes as I was trying to listen to him. In very simple words, he told me what his problems were. It took him a relatively short time to tell me what he thought was relevant or appropriate. Then he became silent. With a minimum of words, he said to me that others were *always right* and that he was *always wrong*; that he was in love with a girl who had left him without explanation; that he was enrolled in the college of engineering but was unable to sit for exams; that he was the last of four brothers and that his father died before he was five. He elaborated a little more in telling me that high school had been a torture for him. He could not understand why history was relevant (as everything was about the past), or why poems are beautiful (so strange, and difficult to decipher), or why philosophy is interesting (when the next thinker regularly contradicts the preceding one). His only peace of mind lay in mathematics and physics, where no one could prove him wrong or stupid. He had never had a good discussion and not even a good argument with any of the boys in his class. He reasoned that he would be happy studying engineering, but it was not so after all, because he could not actually take exams. He said that he was feeling cut away from any hypothetical, incomprehensible spontaneity. And then Percival stopped talking.

Percival was silent not only for minutes or for the rest of the session. He was silent for whole subsequent sessions, and not just for a few days; he was silent for weeks and weeks, certainly over a month and a half. During this very, very long period we sat in my office looking at each other. Of course, I tried every possible way to make him talk, even though trying not to be *too* insistent or intrusive. But he politely and quietly responded that he had no episodes to report, no significant encounters to discuss, no dreams he could remember, no preoccupations, recollections, worries, or fantasies. After more than a month and a half of silence facing each other, although always looking at him, I began to think my own thoughts about a very exciting project I was developing and which had nothing to do with Percival: *The Other Side of Language: A Philosophy of Listening*. He suddenly blushed, became nearly purple-faced, his breathing was accelerating, and tears were welling up in his eyes. Remorseful and embarrassed, I asked him what was happening, what he had thought and how he was feeling. He politely refused to make any comments and I decided not to insist too much.

After another fifteen days of virtual silence, I had to cope with increasing preoccupations about my own technique, capacities, training, and inner world. But then, one day, I became suddenly absorbed in urgently reprioritising my diverse commitments. Once again, Percival nearly cried, profusely perspired, gasped for air, and turned red. Of course, I asked him questions that he did not answer and then I decided to tell him that I had become distracted, that I was thinking about the different errands I had to do, and that I was sorry. With a gentle smile, he said that this can happen to anyone, and that it was not so important. In a later session, after the weekend, he met me at the door with a smile more lively than usual, came into the office, and told me that something happened that had not occurred in a very long time. He had had a dream that felt almost real, even though completely absurd and incomprehensible.

> He was in a bleak, dark slaughterhouse and there was a cow that was about be slaughtered; the attending veterinarian declared that the cow was pregnant and must be spared. A calf was immediately delivered. Then he was in my office where the calf jumped on the desk and began to talk, although he could not understand what the young animal was saying.

Both this time and on subsequent occasions, I did not make any "brilliant" interpretative attempts, or offer psychoanalytic shows. We primarily enjoyed the fact that he indeed was capable of generating dreams, agreed that dreams must come from somewhere inside ourselves, and I encouraged him to express opinions on his dream—if he had any. He told me that there must be some shadowy part of himself to which he had no access, that was always in darkness, that he could not perceive, and that perhaps this part was not so dead or so full of rage; perhaps it did not feel so frightening any more. On this occasion, he also mentioned that he was ashamed for having fallen in love, guilty of feelings that nearly overwhelmed him. He could not understand why so many positive signals had been given by the girl, or why she finally laughed at him and cheerfully dismissed him altogether. As usual, things were just as the *other* proclaimed them to be, and the best he could do was to reproduce what he thought to be an acceptable comment, "You must be right, we are not made for each other." But it was just too difficult when it was a question of strong affects.

Percival shared a large apartment with other students, where they took turns in cleaning and cooking. His kindness bought him time and space with the group. They, of course, took his smile to mean that everything was fine, that he liked them all. No one seemed to notice that his amiable smile meant that he was tense and frozen. No one seemed to care as long as they got what they wanted from him—extra cooking, more cleaning, fixing, repairing. He did not feel assembled enough to assert himself: he had a raging, dead part within himself. He was unable to risk criticism and rejection; as long as the underlying dark part remained unseen, he was constantly tempted to behave in a complacent way, just to relieve the tension, and soldier on. In so doing, he perpetuated his inner split, suffered inauthenticity, and became increasingly burdened with his unlived life. One could say that doing things at this stage was a painful "acting out", not a personal decision. Opting out of one form of distress, he felt as if he was falling into another deeper, more pervasive form of suffering.

In the course of the subsequent analysis, I learnt that one of his most lively childhood memories was that of forcefully holding on to his father in order not to let him go to work. His mother managed a small farm and struggled to bring up the children in a disciplined and efficient way. And now, despite diligently studying his books, he could not bring himself to actually sit for an exam. He said it was a "block". He had learnt to endure sadness and just stay alive. What seemed to be missing was a capacity to realise that he was his own self across very different psychic states (arousal, frustration, calm, and fury), as if this reconnection was just too painful. He felt he did not have the resources to represent and reconnect with his less acceptable mental states. Relations with important others were marred by a fear of violence and abuse to the point that contact with the minds of others was too frightening and dangerous. He had to withdraw, for he could experience safety only in the domain of numbers or of measurable phenomena. This was the only citizenship that entitled him to survive. The shadowy part that he could not see was destined to be forever deadened, obscured and mutely raging. Yet, occasionally, he almost said that if he could only tune into himself he could gain, or regain, some resilience.

At some point, Percival finally sat for his first examination ever, and earned the lowest passing mark: 18. As analysis proceeded, he developed the courage to take more examinations, and each time, almost as if guided by some mathematical model, he regularly earned higher grades. At each examination he increased his marks by two points: 20, 22, 24, 26, 28 and, finally, 30, which is the highest mark. I felt that he was beginning to inhabit and enjoy his own legitimate engineering sanctuary. He believed that his soaring grade average was the result of some calculation, and that was a fact. A sufficiently high grade average would confer the right to postpone military service. At this point, I remarked that, in my view, the *trend* of his grades was the more important element, but no, for him sticking to facts was always empowering. He said that administratively, what really counted was the mathematical average of his grades, not the trend, and he carefully explained to me that in his college there were only engineers and no psychologists.

While he was passing examinations with increasing success, the finances of his family became precarious because of his mother's illness, and he could no longer count on financial help. He decided that he would look around for opportunities to tutor in remedial mathematics for high school children and asked around in different schools if they had students who had problems with maths. Finally, he found a twelve-year old boy who simply could not cope with numbers and geometry. In less than a month, the boy began even to enjoy maths.

Percival had also bought a battered scooter, which he renovated to mechanical perfection, and he managed to find four more pupils, using the scooter to travel around the city to teach them in their homes, fastening it with a chain to lamp-posts while he was tutoring. I asked him how he succeeded in teaching maths so effectively. He said that to begin with, he asked the student to show him his textbook and then he carefully read aloud the sentences in the book, and also sought simpler terms. To his astonishment, his pupils said that it was clear. Then he very carefully wrote the figures—for instance, those of an algebraic equation—in a notebook and then asked the pupil what it was that they could do with that. Different suggestions or possibilities came up and so he asked the pupil to write the one that made sense to *both* of them. He did the same with geometry problems. He made very good drawings, wrote numbers very clearly, and together they tried then to find the first step to solve the riddle. The secret was doing things one step at a time, without skipping any of the steps, and then also enjoying the patently *obvious* conclusion of the exercise. Many more requests came for tutoring as he developed for himself the reputation of a "magic" teacher. But that was also therapeutic for Percival, as he could enliven himself by helping others to break free from their paralyses: mathematics was just like playing with numbers and if you use the right rules, you simply go on playing and eventually winning.

Percival's dreams were still extremely rare, but they came out occasionally. After he had earned the grade of "30", he had this dream: the professor who had given him the top grade had sent him on a research mission to the North Pole where, for some reason, the ice was beginning to melt. His specific task was to measure the temperature in spots where the ice had melted away and the brown earth was beginning to surface.

Percival's scooter was still his only way to move around the city in order to teach maths, which gave him the means to support himself, and pay for his analysis. One day around dusk, he saw a man, whom he vaguely knew, trying to cut the chain that attached his scooter to a lamp-post. His ears became burning hot and his heartbeat quickened. Driven by an impetus of strange, cold rage, he pushed the man away, causing him to drop his bolt-cutters to the ground. When the would-be thief reacted aggressively, Percival gave him a severe beating. The other responded clumsily and only just managed to escape the punishment Percival was meting out. After a while, Percival calmed down and continued to his next maths lesson. He did not feel guilty; on the contrary, he felt fine.

Confronting the shadow

The attempt here is to provide elements of integration in support of the notion of the "shadow", an essential and elusive aspect of our inner organisation. Why should we revisit this topic and try to reaffirm its relevance? Primarily because contacts with our shadow can be very challenging and even psychically painful. The reconnection with this part of the self can give rise to fear, but is definitely necessary—productive, in fact. Dealing with this issue, however distressing, seems essential for the success of any attempt to move forward creatively in our life journey. Bringing our shadow out requires working with our largely hidden, secluded self. If we do not do this, we risk being absorbed by it, identifying with it, or, even worse, we might refuse to acknowledge it altogether. We need instead to turn the shadow into a partner. When the shadow becomes one's partner, its function is somehow changed. Without this connection, the shadow remains nothing more than the accumulation of our "worst" tendencies. The shadow is repugnant to us and our fear of it is understandable. And perhaps some of us might even remember a troubled time in life when the shadow nearly overwhelmed us. At times like this, one has been dragged into the shadow, as if it had hijacked one's life. Why are integration and spontaneity so difficult to reach? It is almost as if inside each one of us there is a *second* self, a living being we are deeply ashamed of. No matter how hard we try, we can never get rid of this doppelgänger, our shadow. It is, in fact, the embodiment of everything that is offensive to us, everything we do not want to be but fear we are. It is probably called the shadow because it is with us wherever we go. Jung was perhaps the first to say that everyone has a shadow, regardless of their manifest talents, success, and psychic attitude. It is regarded as an archetype, but there is a way in which the shadow is different from all the other archetypes that affect how you see the world: the shadow determines how you see yourself.

Contact with one's shadow is invariably problematic. By way of illustration, in one of Anne Brontë's novels we find an imaginative rendition of what it could be like to attempt this contact. We may wish to *see* the whole truth in our personality and also to tell it, for truth always conveys its own meaning to those who are able to receive it. Yet, as the priceless treasure of truth often lies hidden at the bottom of a well, it needs some courage to dive for it, especially as the one who does so will probably incur more scorn and repugnance for the mud and water into which he or she has had to plunge than thanks for the jewel retrieved. In like fashion, when we undertake the cleaning of a dirty, cluttered place, there is more likelihood that we will be abused because of the dust raised than thanked for the cleaning (Brontë, 1994, p. 18). In fact, for those conditioned to seem reflexively good or compliant, the flight from the shadow also, paradoxically, becomes the flight from one's more vital part of the self. A shadowless person is a contradiction in terms. One who believes that we have no shadow can be very superficial and quite prone to damage him or herself and others. In Hollis's view, to the question, "What, then, is my shadow?", we could answer,

> Whatever within us we wish not to face, but which nonetheless carries the germ of our wholeness . . . and renews its course in our life through sundry disguises such as projection onto others, repression of a vital part of ourselves, or as the narrowing of life. (Hollis, 2003, p. 47)

These disguises can turn us into a caricature of our own self. Many of those who are caught in the "virtue trap"—those conditioned to appear reflexively good and compliant—do not appear to be self-destructive to the casual eye. Bent on being good spouses, good parents, good children, or whatever, they may construct a false self that looks admirable to the world and meets with a great deal of worldly approval. This false, constricted self is always patient, always willing to meet the demands of another, and yet can be gravely unintegrated—ultimately a caricature.

Yet, the shadow cannot simply be evil, for it is a requisite element of wholeness. A profound understanding of the self is based on the encounter with that which challenges the ego. The shadow thus becomes the source of one of the most basic human conflicts. Because we are ashamed of our shadow, we look outside of ourselves for some evidence of our worth. This constantly takes the form of looking to others for approval and validation—in a state of dependence, in fact. Then, since we are hiding the shadow, the external forces cause us to "freeze". If we painstakingly try to accept our shadow we tend to defreeze because we are no longer terrorised by potential observers. Also, our higher self might have its own dignity that is not dependent on the approval of others. In fact, the entire advertising world preys on our need for acceptance. If you acquire a certain product, you will be accepted, loved, and taken up by the best people; if you do not, you are stuck—alone with your shameful shadow.

From a psychoanalytic perspective, suffering is not merely the product of incorrect perceptions produced by a defective mind, as if saying we should change our distorted thinking patterns and our painful feelings will disappear, tantamount to saying that an early, incorrect assessment of reality produced the inner pain. What I have referred to as anaesthetics (that is, remedies or relations that dull the discomfort of an underlying problem), are not the only means of avoiding suffering. In fact, we can anaesthetise ourselves in a further and more damaging way: by psychologically severing parts of our psyche that are too painful or too intractable for us (Davies, 2012, p. 130). Perhaps we could resort to William James to enlighten us on this point. For instance: "The method of averting attention from evil and living simply in the light of good is splendid as long as it works" (James, 1985, quoted in Davies, 2012, p. 132). Also, our sloganised power of positive thinking is essentially inadequate "because the evil facts which it refuses positively to account for are a genuine portion of reality" (James, 1985, quoted in Davies, 2012, p. 132), inner and outer. In Jung's view, the idea that anything could be real or true which does not come from outside has barely begun to dawn on contemporary culture. He adds,

Not that "psychic forces" have anything to do with the conscious mind, fond as we are of playing with the idea that consciousness and psyche are identical. This is only another piece of intellectual presumption. "Psychic forces" have far more to do with the realm of the unconscious. (Jung, 1936, p. 185)

Thus, we must necessarily come to terms with our shadowy self.

The ongoing sense that problems are meaningful indicates a fundamental difference between the basic attitude of consumers, as contrasted to the attitude of creators. Perhaps behind the rejection of any *other* person is a deeper rejection of a part of one's own self. And the shadow is almost a separate being living inside us. Perhaps the feelings we have for "others" stem from our feelings towards this hidden part of ourselves. Until one can accept this part of the self, there is no accepting the other. As is known, just as each of us is divided against himself, similarly society at large is divided by different groups operating against one other. In Jung's gaze, it suits our hypertrophied and hubristic modern consciousness not to be mindful of the dangerous autonomy of the unconscious and to treat it negatively as an absence of consciousness (Jung, 1936, p. 185).

The default of projective strategies

The thesis here is that if we could develop a capacity to endure contact with our shadow, we could perhaps break free, at least partially, from the repetitive and illusory strategies of projection. Forever designating external bearers of our most intractable parts, we automatically react to frustrations by means of projections. Monotonous, reactive projections may ultimately damage our capacity for psychic actions. To escape this paralysis, we probably need allies. If we could create a legitimate, respected epistemic space for the complex question of psychic pain, we could increasingly count on the constructive empathy of fellow sufferers. I am trying to delineate something that is currently a mere potential, and yet, it could irrevocably come to exist once it is generally accepted: empathy (not sympathy, of course) for the others' psychic tribulation.

As is known, among the most useful, if the most misunderstood, of Jung's contributions to psychology is the idea of the shadow (Jung,

1951, p. 9). In Jung's view, the shadow is everything about oneself with which one is uncomfortable. One might not be conscious of one's shadow, or one might not wish to be conscious of it, for it is whatever one does not want to be. As an illusory defence, we project it on to others and repudiate in them what is intolerable so close to home. In Jung's comprehensive view,

> Although, with insight and good will, the shadow can to some extent be assimilated into the conscious personality, experience shows that there are certain features which offer the most obstinate resistance to moral control and prove almost impossible to influence. These resistances are usually bound up with *projections*, which are not recognized as such, and their recognition is a moral achievement beyond the ordinary. While some traits peculiar to the shadow can be recognized without too much difficulty as one's own personal qualities, in some cases both insight and good will are unavailing because the emotion appears to lie, beyond all possibility of doubt, within the *other* person. No matter how obvious it may be to the neutral observer that it is a matter of projections, there is little hope that the subject will perceive this himself. (Jung, 1951, p. 10)

From a very clear clinical perspective, Jung adds a compassionate, alarming comment:

> It is often tragic to see how blatantly a man bungles his own life and the lives of others yet remaining totally incapable of seeing how much the whole tragedy originates in himself, and continually he feeds it and keeps it going. (Jung, 1951, p. 10)

A similar view is expressed by Symington, where he points out the paradoxical attitude of some subjects:

> In the person who is most passive, most jelly-like, there is at the same time the most virulent projective identification . . . It is very common for someone who is very passive to be surrounded by people who are exasperated with him. (Symington, 2002, p. 62)

This deficiency forces the individual into an adhesive constriction of others in the attempt to avoid the burden of psychic pain and to place its provenance into others. By means of psychic intrusion, this strategy seems to become even simpler.

As is known, people attempt to change external reality without any prior reorganisation of their inner organisation. We make plans without taking into account the blueprint for dysfunction that every human being carries within himself. In theory, one could even renew projections repeatedly. Idealisations could also be drawn into the dynamics: the right person is out there, someone who will free us, succour us, parent us. The *right* job, the *right* home, the *right* ideology could be there, just over the next horizon. Ferro insists that in paranoid disorders intolerable aspects of the self are spread among others who become persecutory custodians of these aspects. Sometimes, these bearers are picked at random and according to chance; at other times, they are sought in the same way as a film director seeks an actor for a special part by a careful process of casting (Ferro, 2011, p. 36). But what if we could partially, provisionally, become capable of tolerating these intolerable parts of our self? What if we could learn to endure this pain and not be paralysed by it to the point of having to force it into others? What would happen if we accepted our aliens and learnt to negotiate with them, instead of just projecting the terror? My answer is that there is no final solution, but only a beneficial process of moving forward, and that a condition of permanent incapacity to move on is very close to psychic death. Ferro also remarks that in ordinary life we usually both project and contain. In this context, we regard projective identification as a basic activity of the human mind. In therapy, most projective identifications flow from patient to analyst, but this is not always the case:

> Sometimes the flow can be reversed and a tired (occluded), (unavailable) or suffering analyst may evacuate anxieties into the mind of the patient, and in these cases his mind temporarily takes on the function of a receptive-dreaming hub. (Ferro, 2011, p. 63)

A dialogue based on authentic listening usually involves some discomfort, friction, and pain, which is the price for actually communicating. When all of this cannot be endured, we automatically anaesthetise the dialogue; we dull the dialogue by transforming it into criticism of distant others, any others, made into the bearers of something too horrible to say or to hear. Thus, we induce the exhilarating pleasure of secretly joining with our interlocutors in playing at projective identification—ultimately a collusive, benumbing game. It is a passive but devastating manoeuvre that might occasion sympathy, but certainly not empathy. The point is that it is common to oscillate between consciousness and shadow, from one extreme to the other, without ever trying to put the two together. It is either one or the other, never both. When we are made to perceive this, we find it almost unbearable. Add to this the ego's tendency to dissociate from that which is uncomfortable or too challenging and it is no wonder, then, that the shadow remains so elusive.

The meaning of human suffering is by no means easily deciphered while our remarkable capacity for consciousness remains both our blessing and our torment. Most of our problems tend to be explained by means of projections, in terms of the malevolence of the environment—a vicious circle whereby our isolation is intensified. According to Jung, the effect of projection is to isolate the subject from his surroundings, since the result is an illusory relation to it, instead of a real one:

> Projections change the world into the replica of one's own unknown face. In the last analysis, therefore, they lead to an autoerotic or autistic condition in which one dreams a world whose reality remains forever unattainable. (Jung, 1951, p. 9)

If we could be helped to bear the pain of the acceptance of our shadow, we could perhaps break free from such an illusion. As we shall see, the famous character of Dr Jekyll illusorily believes that he can freely shift from integration to fragmentation in order to avoid all psychic pain and safeguard his immaculate medical reputation. With her customary acumen, Midgley suggests that the acknowledged shadow may be terrible enough, but it is the unacknowledged one which is the killer (Midgley, 1984, p. 122). In fact, Jekyll has not so much become two persons as *ceased* to be a person. Conversely, the specificity of our talent for healing is to endure the painful struggles of inner connectedness instead of falling into "exhilarating" projective inclinations, because, of course, we can only project what we have previously disconnected. In Jung's words,

> The Shadow is a moral problem that challenges the whole . . . personality, for no one can become conscious of the Shadow without considerable moral effort. To become conscious of it involves recognizing the dark aspects of the personality as present and real. This act is the

essential condition for any kind of self-knowledge, and it therefore, as a rule, meets with considerable resistance. Indeed, self-knowledge as a psychotherapeutic measure requires much painstaking work extending over a long period. (Jung, 1951, p. 8)

But, then, how painstaking does it have to be? And, can we afford all that?

Probably the worst of human conditions are not met with in our psychoanalytic settings; also, clinical material is often attenuated to some extent. In this connection, we could think of a creative novelist as being a "reporter" of inner events in the life of characters. From this perspective, we could agree with a significant suggestion by Anne Brontë: she remarks that even with extravagant over-colouring of parts that are carefully copied from life, an author may go too far. When we have to do with vicious fictional characters, it is better to depict them as they really are, rather than as they would wish to appear. To present a bad thing in its least offensive light is, doubtless, the most agreeable course for a writer of fiction, but is it the most honest, or the safest? (Brontë, 1994, p. 18). If we were not whispering to ourselves that all is well when it is not, there would be less misery for the young ones who are left to extract their knowledge that all cannot always be well from experience. It is certainly true that we can acquire knowledge from experience, but the "I" of our personality could function as the silent witness of both experience and of our projective furores. If the "I" of our personality could be seen as a receptive self, as an embracing witness that rests beneath the mind states activated in our daily lives, we could be relatively ready to receive whatever arrives from the outer and inner world, inviting all aspects of our selves into its shelter. In Ferro's outlook, this is the function of an interpretative setting, for, in fact, this ideal situation is hard to achieve in isolation.

To avoid being hijacked by our shadow, the inner observer must work with the shadow at its best, rather than possibly collapsing into it. Inner security demands that we endure the psychic pain of dealing with the shadow and ultimately of making it an associate in our life's venture. Without this rather difficult association, the shadow remains nothing more than the sum total of the worst aspects of our personality. Yet, the moment we achieve an ongoing relationship with the shadow, a range of creative possibilities seems to open for us. If I deny my shadow, I am certainly ignorant, but if I cannot see the opportunities that it involves, then I am crippled—that is, psychically paralysed. Inner struggling does not diminish our inner life, but makes it stronger. I think that it is heroic and loving to acknowledge that what is repeatedly stuck in our relationships dwells within ourselves. Such a recognition is creative in the sense that it requires enormous strength to take on the psychic burden of one's shadow, rather than trying to make others into what we need: external bearers of our shadow. Also, it is quite loving because it frees others from the burden of carrying our own psychic agendas.

Feeling intensely connected to one's shadow gives one an inner sense of confidence, for it eliminates the fear of being exposed, the fear of any inner or outer audience. It is when we try to hide our shadow that we become truly terrified of the audience. If we could embrace the shadow, it could actually be a major relief. Perhaps, when we join together the forces of our conscious self and of our shadow, we will not end up with a diminished, shadowy version of our own self. We develop a *whole*, which is more than the sum of two parts. Paradoxically, the best part in us, the highest version of ourselves, is only at work when we are in an ongoing partnership with our shadow. It almost feels as if some alchemical transformation is going on. In Winnicott's view, if we cannot bear the mental strain of paradoxes (Winnicott, 1971, p. xii), we relapse into uncreative attitudes. In his *Mysterium Coniunctionis*, Jung emphasises the tremendous roles that the opposites and their union play in alchemy and helps us understand why alchemists were so fond of paradoxes. In order to attain this union, they tried not only to visualise the opposites together, but to describe them in a single expression, in the same breath. Jung quotes a few of them: "I am the black of the white . . ."; or, "The principle of art is the raven, who flies without wings in the blackness of night and in the brightness of day"; or, "Burn in water and wash in fire". And further, "Seek the coldness of the moon and you shall find the heat of the sun" (Jung, 1955, p. 43).

Dr Jekyll: a case that is not so strange

To explore the shadow and demonstrate the valuable use of psychic pain, we shall invoke here a very popular "clinical" example derived from a classic novel: *The Strange Case of Dr Jekyll and Mr Hyde* (Stevenson, 2002). In varying degrees of severity, the basic paradigm of the case is not so strange, and, in fact, quite common in everyday life. As is known, Dr Jekyll recognises early in life that his medical ambitions are in conflict with his inclination to dissolute behaviour. Thus, he manages to separate the two aspects of his personality so that each can pursue its interests without the interference of the other. Quite smart. He seems to embrace the view that to avoid all inner pain, a human being does not have to be truly one, but can actually be two, or even more. But, of course, Dr Jekyll, the respected physician, does not think of this as a dangerous venture requiring a drastic disconnection, but, rather, as an equal distribution of power between the two parts, perhaps functioning on a time-sharing basis. The clever Dr Jekyll simply regards this expedient as a sign of brilliance that will allow him the pleasures of dissipation while safeguarding his social image. A nice trick, functioning on the assumption that it does not matter what you do with the shadowy parts of your self, but this is, in fact, a misleading hypothesis, based on the incorrect understanding of inner splitting. At first obsequious, the segregated part may rapidly grow increasingly intrusive and eventually subjugate the apparently pristine aspect of its creator in the role of its servant. When resisted, it might even kill.

Midgley also points out that when we look for someone who conceived a self-damaging splitting strategy, we cannot find one at all (Midgley, 1984, p. 122). Why? Because when we seem to have found one, we often find parts of the self with no connection to one another. And that "person" may appear perfectly sincere, while lying all the time. The segregated parts always lie when speaking for the individual, whole person—forever both innocent and wicked. In the case of Dr Jekyll, splitting is meant as an anaesthetising device that avoids painful contacts and difficult negotiations. But perhaps the trick is too successful, too smart. As we only have one brain, no matter how much splitting there is to avoid pain, the fact remains that both Dr Jekyll and Mr Hyde live inside the same skull/brain. The difficulties that ensue are ultimately more damaging than the pains one is trying to avoid.

In Stevenson's view, Mr Hyde is Jekyll's twin, shadow, or *doppelgänger*, the embodiment of evil that freely goes around performing crime in his stead (Stevenson, 2002, p. 5). If we try not to acknowledge its existence—refuse, that is, to accept our shadow, and deny it—it forcibly reacts, and our battle is lost: we are doomed to succumb, just as Dr Jekyll did. The intensity of Stevenson's language leads me to extract a sequence of quotes that give incisive illustrations of the problem of splitting. Reading his book, we wait in suspense for the thin veil of respectability to be drawn aside when we can finally look into the realm of violence. The sense of a lurking presence haunts the atmosphere, as disquieting as the presence of wickedness in the soul of Dr Jekyll. We read,

> Though so profound a double dealer, I was in no sense a hypocrite; both sides of me were in dead earnest; I was no more myself when I laid aside restraint and plunged into shame, than when I laboured, in the eye of the day, at the furtherance of knowledge or the relief of sorrow and suffering. (Stevenson, 2002, p. 100)

Dr Jekyll continues in this way:

> I had learned to dwell with pleasure, as a beloved daydream, on the thought of the separation of these elements. If each, I told myself, could be housed in separate identities, life would be relieved of all that was unbearable; the unjust could go his way, delivered from the aspirations and remorse of his more upright twin. (Stevenson, 2002, p. 101)

Further on:

> Hence, although I had now two characters as well as two appearances, one was wholly evil, and the other was still the old Henry Jekyll, that incongruous component of whose reformation and improvement I had already learned to despair. The movement was thus wholly toward the worse. (Stevenson, 2002, p. 107)

Jekyll concludes, "I have learned that the burden of our life is for ever on man's shoulders; and when the attempt is made to cast it off, it but returns upon us with more unfamiliar and more awful pressure" (Stevenson, 2002, p. 102). So, the crux of the problem is the propensity to regard splitting as an innocuous trick, whereas it ultimately amounts to damaging one's own self. According to Symington, "An action whereby I smash up my own mind is the archetypal evil, and this action of its nature fashions unconsciousness" (Symington, 2004, p. 65). In a vicious spiral, unconsciousness is also attained in order not to suffer the self-damaging hurt that we perpetrate.

CHAPTER FIVE

The relational outlook

Winnicott and Hegel on personal confrontations

To circumscribe Winnicott's contributions to the well-defined discipline of child psychoanalysis would be to miss his acumen and intellectual scope. Phillips reminds us, in fact, that for Winnicott it was not a question of what was real about human beings, which would presuppose some known essence, but of what, for each person, "gives the feeling of real" (Phillips, 1988, p. 127). This can only be found by each person within in his or her self. This outlook encourages the pursuit of personal involvement in the challenge of *inner* growth. *Outer* growth *per se* could be quite puzzling: getting bigger and bigger without ever growing in our mind. As we know, modern analysts think first in terms of relationships and, second, in terms of instinctual satisfaction, somehow reversing the historical psychoanalytic sequence. Object relations theorists believe that, from the beginning of life, human beings are seeking relationships and not merely instinctual satisfaction. An involvement in relation, however difficult, can make it possible for the developing subject to attain a level where creative dynamics are possible, although, of course, not guaranteed, in the way of repeated painstaking attempts to "feel real". Thus, we primarily think of maturation in terms of interpersonal vicissitudes. In some early stages of psychoanalytic culture, it was widely assumed that if a person was happy and healthy, there must also be the enjoyment of a satisfying sexual life; and, conversely, if a person was neurotically unhappy, there must be a disturbance in the capacity for sexual relations. Perhaps, during Freud's lifetime, the main emphasis was on instinctual satisfaction (Storr, 1997, p. 3). It was tacitly implied that if partners were able to give each other satisfaction in the sexual domain, other aspects of their relationship would probably function well. According to Storr, "Sex was the touchstone by which the whole relationship could be evaluated" (Storr, 1997, p. 3). Now, commonly, we have come to believe that sexual relations are to be integrated with, or should emanate from, a complex interpersonal condition.

Phillips points out that, for Winnicott, talking about mothers and babies was a way of saying things about partners (dyads, couples), that he would not otherwise have been able to say. It is not that Winnicott is not really talking about mothers and babies, but that he is also using parents and infants to talk about still other kinds of relations (Phillips, 1988, p. ix). Winnicott is also concerned with sexuality and with a person's relation with one's own self. "And the writing, above all, is not dogmatic, not full of conviction, it is not essentialist but pragmatic", remarks Phillips (1988, p. ix). We could even use the present continuous tense (or gerund) in such a way as to indicate what we are trying to do with whatever partner we are involved with. If asked, "What are you doing?", we could perhaps answer by saying that, for instance, we are mothering, fathering, wifeing, husbanding, mastering, or slaving. Of course, we could also say that we are analysing or patienting. Phillips points out that Winnicott, ultimately, is most interested in what it might be like to be "very much a person", to be alive as one might have it in oneself to be so (Phillipps, 1988, p. x). From this perspective, we could perhaps point to parallels, or even convergences, with Hegel's celebrated dialectics of emblematic figures such as lords and bondsmen, masters and slaves (Hegel, 1977, p. 111).

Of course, the question of interpersonal knowledge cannot be confined to occasional intellectual debates. It is, rather, a situation that we live out daily in our moment-by-moment interactions, and our living it out occurs with or without our awareness. A Hegel–Winnicott juxtaposition is hardly scandalising or inappropriate—what is scandal, after all? Certainly, there is a tremendous distance in terms of background and scope, but there are commonalities, too: Hegel and Winnicott are very different, talented humans, very much concerned with what humans try to do. Winnicott's speaking of mothers and babies can be reconnected to *any* critical interpersonal relation in which we can transform our primarily biological condition into a psychic, dialogical situation. (It could be seen as the celebrated Hegelian transition from the "thing in itself" into the ulterior domain of the "thing for oneself", and for "ourselves".) The enlightening emphasis on the exploration of paradigms in interpersonal relations might incline us to revisit a seminal piece of writing of our western tradition. The basic question is, what happens when people try to interact and grow—or grow and interact? Is there perhaps a general paradigm that could apply to a variety of situations? Certainly, Hegel has made such an attempt. Just as Winnicott was not only talking about mothers and babies, Hegel was not just talking about "bondsmen" and "lords". The acumen of Winnicott's insights could, perhaps, in part coincide with Hegel's well known *Phenomenology of the Spirit*, Part IV "The truth of self certainty", especially with Section A, titled "Independence and dependence of self consciousness: lordship and bondage" (Hegel, 1977, p. 111). This text could be seen as some kind of tentative paradigm for the dynamics of interpersonal relations and for their emancipatory value. If we regard the "slave" as an emblematic figure standing for whoever has insufficient or no negotiation power in whatever situation (even comparable to the condition of the helpless baby expressed in the Freudian notion of *Hilflosigkeit*), and if we regard the "master" as anyone having disproportionate or absolute power in a relation (comparable to an archaic parent full of milk and might), we might look at the Hegelian text as potentially applying to disparate situations. Just as Winnicott is "using mothers and babies to talk about other things as well", Hegel speaks about masters and slaves to illustrate a variety of comparable situations. It is worth noting that the dialectics of mastery–servitude can inaccurately be understood as a practice of taking turns in the exercise of power, a practice which would impede the opportunity to gradually metamorphose relations into more creative and maturational processes. What if patriarchy only repeated the horrors of matriarchy—as if it were a long-term way of taking turns?

If we could modulate our collective horror of inner pain we could perhaps more easily opt for the psychic actions in which repetition compulsion *no longer* is the deadening, subjacent rule. If we remain incapable of inner actions we can only opt for outer actions, such as, for instance, eliminating Laius or Oedipus, lords or bondsmen. In my view, the whole dialectic between master and slave is all about becoming capable of inner actions, of managing to move from reactions to actions. The point is to try to resolve the burden of our human coexistence by making it more versatile and creative, overcoming the fixity of roles and moving on to more mature psychic interactions. In Hegel's assessment of the paradigmatic vicissitudes occurring between master and slave, a transformational dynamic is somehow envisioned ad advocated.

Braving Hegel's "antiquated" language, we could read that

> Self-consciousness exists in and for itself when . . . it so exists for another; that is it exists only in being acknowledged. . . . Its moments, then, must on the one hand be held strictly apart, and on the other must in this differentiation at the same time also be taken and known as not distinct, or in their opposite significance. (Hegel, 1977, p. 111)

Indeed, a sufficiently clear statement of mission and scope. In psychoanalytic terms, we could say that at the beginning of psychic life, self-definition, the awareness of existing as a separate person and the development of a coherent identity, is rooted in recognition and depends, therefore, on interaction. And, of course, from our psychoanalytic perspective, we are used to speaking of parents and children, therapists and patients. In Hegel's view, "The action has a double significance not only because it is directed against itself as well as against the other, but also because it is indivisibly the action of one as well as of the other" (Hegel, 1977, p. 112). Similarly, in therapeutic vicissitudes, it is often the case of the twofold significance of psychic actions. From a Kleinian perspective, our very early vicissitudes could perhaps be described in terms of *phantasy* reciprocal actions. Could we say that the Kleinian notion of "phantasy" is comparable to precocious psychic action? I believe that Gaddini would have embraced this hypothesis. We might even, in fact, observe our primitive presentations of contrast and struggle. According to Hegel, in these primitive vicissitudes,

> This presentation is a twofold action: action on the part of the other, and action on its own part. In so far as it is the action of the *other*, each seeks the death of the other. But in doing so, the second kind of action, action on its own part, is also involved; for the former involves the staking of its own life. (Hegel, 1977, p. 113)

This is a capacity of total commitment, of accepting the challenge, even if tremblingly. Winnicott repeatedly asks whether this is outright hatred or just primitive love. It is true that a parent is very powerful with respect to an infant, but he also uses the infant to prove his own might and existential necessity (and in this sense he is somehow dependent upon the infant). But this can be a static and repetitive situation; what is ultimately relevant is its dialectical interaction, the staking of one's whole inner life for the sake of one's transition from dependence to freedom.

> Thus the relationship of the two [potential] self-conscious individuals is that they prove themselves and each other through a life-and-death struggle. They must engage in this struggle, for they must raise their certainty of being *for themselves* to truth, both in the case of the other and in their own case. And it is only through staking one's life that freedom is won. (Hegel, 1977, p. 113)

Freedom from what? Perhaps from the fixity of an archaic psychic position, of a role, that impedes renovation and movement. The terror and trembling of the infant and his survival of it affirm his being a creative subject capable of surviving death and, thus, acquiring a "right" to challenge the omnipotent lord/master/parent. All this primarily happens in the domain of *inner* actions.

Terms such as relationship, interaction, connection, and confrontation are used to connote a very modern, democratic approach to our human condition. Yet, a psychoanalytic setting could hardly be imagined as a comfortable room in which two adults are civilly exchanging points of view. It is not. Winnicott frequently points out vicissitudes of psychic "hatred" and of a will to survive both in primordial relations and in a psychoanalytic contexts. Winnicott also occasionally makes reference to the vicious lullabies mothers sing to their babies who, fortunately, do not understand the words. Yalom mentions one:

> Rockabye, Baby, on the treetop,
> When the wind blows the cradle will rock,
> When the bough breaks the cradle will fall,
> And down will come baby, cradle and all.
>
> (Yalom, 2011, p. 219)

This lullaby might be emblematic of all the sadistic nonsense that can be poured into the children as a maladroit way of alleviating the adults' troubled inner world.

In Hegel's words, "The individual who has not risked his life may well be recognised as a person, but he has not attained to the truth of this recognition as an independent self consciousness" (Hegel, 1977, p. 114). Paradoxically, it is our tendency to settle for some "adapted life" that can induce the performance of repetitive destructive acts. Destructiveness could then be understood as the result of our tendency to conformity and adaptation to circumstances that do not permit the expression of higher psychic developments. Yet, again, we can reflect on how painful it can be to give up the benefits of certainty (for instance, the assurance that the villain has been eliminated) in both lordship and servitude. But then, outer actions, or simply reactions, do not generate maturity. Both Laius, in trying to eliminate Oedipus, *and* Oedipus, in eliminating Laius, have performed reactive, psychically uncreative, non-maturational actions. What is demanded is something in the way of inner actions. In Hegel's view, by avoiding the struggle of a dialectic confrontation, by resigning to adaptation,

> There vanishes from their interplay the essential moment of splitting into extremes with opposite characteristics; and the middle term collapses in a lifeless unity which is split into lifeless, merely immediate, unopposed extremes; and the two do not reciprocally give and receive one another back from each other consciously, but leave each other only indifferently, like things. (Hegel, 1977, p. 114)

And here is the Hegelian refrain: "Their act is an abstract negation, not the negation coming from consciousness, which supersedes in such a way as to preserve and maintain what is superseded, and consequently survives its own supersession" (Hegel, 1977, p. 114).

Once again, Hegel points out the potential function of negative, painful experiences:

> But this objective negative moment is none other than the alien being before which it has trembled. Now, however, he destroys this alien negative moment, posits himself as a negative in the . . . order of things and thereby becomes for himself, someone existing on his own account. (Hegel, 1977, p. 118)

Thus we are regularly to reconfigure our relationship to our suffering. We could experiment with personal vicissitudes that convince us that suffering, however frightening, might, in fact, transform us for the better. Or it might ultimately serve our interests, intimating that radical change, inner change, is necessary. At any rate, this sort of thinking confirms us as the protagonists of challenging events. If it becomes too taxing, then we can even struggle to win empathic allies to fight with. Still another paradox: the sense of being a suffering protagonist also supports the conviction that the suffering is definitely temporary. To feel truly real, as Winnicott says, our famous psychoanalytic objects must ultimately become real subjects. To recapitulate: the master can only be a subject because the slave incarnates the thing-like object that recognises him as master; in this way, the potential subjectivity of whoever is in power is dependent upon the powerless one. A lord frees himself from this dependence upon the bondsman by allowing for mutual recognition, rather than a one-way recognition: only because he is a slave can I be a master. This essential paradigmatic dynamic can repeat itself in the most disparate interpersonal conditions. The terms "slave" and "master" are only used as linguistic instruments to articulate common human vicissitudes.

Non-recognition is a self-deadening, repetitive disaster related to our insufficient capacity for psychic actions. We could be tempted to remark, about our emblematic Freudian heroes, if only Laius had not tried to kill Oedipus, or, if only Oedipus had not killed Laius. Phillips reminds us that Winnicott "believes in the possibility of the non-collusive life, of being in his words 'isolated without being insulated'" (Phillips, 1988, p. xiii). Health, for Winnicott, is to do with the mutuality of relationship. Without a very hard-won "mutuality of relationship", we remain enslaved to repetitions–retaliations that can be either immediate or distanced in time, sometimes for decades, and which leave things just as they are. Unless facts, historical occurrences, or relational events are somehow metamorphosed into psychic, thinkable vicissitudes, there can only be repetition, or tragedy, forever impeding inner growth.

Empathic allies and the fixity of roles

We should be realistic and objective enough, ultimately humble enough, to accept inner pain and not abhor it to the point of becoming paralysed by the acute shame of inner suffering. We should also be well aware of the mythic nature of the "fully analysed healthy therapist" (Yalom, 2011, p. 8). No analyst, indeed, no person, can be immune to the inherent suffering of our *human* condition. In fact, there is nothing rhetorical or merely symbolic about struggling through life, for that is what we constantly do. Conversely, we could ultimately lapse into a dangerous, risky parody of inner life. By way of illustration, I shall invoke a short story of Herman Hesse's (Hesse, 1990). Through a simple, emblematic story, something like a *midrash*, he tells us of Joseph and Dion, two highly regarded healers/physicians/psychotherapists of antiquity. Joseph was the younger of the two and his therapeutic methods were rooted in tireless listening and inspirational comments. Sufferers developed a total trust in him: psychic pain and distress poured into him and vanished like water in the desert's sand. Consulting "pilgrims" attending his clinic left his presence detoxified and serene.

Quite different from Joseph, the older healer, Dion, confronted those who came for help in a directive way. He cured through active interventions, potions, and specific recommendations. The two doctors had never met, even though they worked as "rivals" in the collective imagination of their time. But then, all of a sudden, Joseph became "spiritually" ill, fell into despair, and was tormented by ideas of self-destruction. Totally unable to cure himself with his own methods, he humbly and bravely set out on a journey to find the famous Dion and seek *his* masterful help. On the very long journey towards Dion, Joseph rested one night at a crowded oasis, where he struck up conversation with a tired traveller. When Joseph finally revealed the purpose of his journey, the other traveller offered himself as a guide in his search for Dion. Towards the end of their long journey the other traveller revealed to Joseph that he himself was Dion—the very healer that Joseph was seeking. Without hesitation, Dion invited his younger and despairing colleague into his home; Joseph accepted becoming his assistant, and they worked together for years. In the end, Joseph returned to his home and practice.

Years later, Dion fell ill and believed that this would be his final illness. On his deathbed, he succeeded in summoning his younger colleague. Now that he was dying, Dion said to Joseph that the hour had come to reveal that when they first met in the oasis, the encounter had seemed a miracle to him, for he, too, had fallen into a devastating illness and was on his way to Joseph to seek his help because he was unable to cure himself with any of his specific remedies. This is to say that of course they were prestigious healers, but, primarily, they were fellow sufferers, staunch travellers, and humble seekers of help. Not only did the two highly regarded psycho-physicians endure a reversal of roles from healer to sufferer, but also could overcome the disciplinary identifications that are frequently used for the attainment of clinical certitude and for the reduction of anxiety—the sort of convictions that we often use as anaesthetising aids.

In Davies' view, a shameful vision of suffering prevails in our culture and consequently induces unproductive attitudes and the repeated use of anaesthetics: "This fact constitutes one of the most damaging results of the negative vision's ascent in recent decades" (Davies, 2012, p. 165). Yet, ultimately, the battle against uncreative suffering can be too strenuous for lonely, isolated fighters. The "alchemic" transmutation of inner pain into creative suffering can be more realistically attempted in an atmosphere of empathy rooted in authentic listening—as in the case of Joseph and Dion. If higher education could be viewed as an indicator of our times, we could perhaps notice that in their advertising brochures, virtually one hundred per cent of the pictures represent fully smiling figures, as if to convey the silent message that nothing as obscene as psychic pain could be found in the admirable institution. They proclaim, in fact, that they offer the most powerful anaesthetics: networking and success. These anaesthetics might seldom work, and so we become ensnared in the vicious circle of the unremitting search for guaranteed absence of pain. As in the case of Oedipus, the need to be a great and powerful man (to compensate, perhaps, for his foundling origin) makes it hard for him to be an ordinary adult man. When parents are despising and abusive (or even murderous, as in the case of Oedipus), one's personal growth is an unbearable challenge to such parents, and so an even harsher reaction is to be expected from them. Also, we erroneously believe that we should do something truly extraordinary if we are thinking of emancipation. And, of course, our first uncertain steps may be derided. One might even feel ridiculous in trying to appear like an adult and to feel so helpless as to venture on a lonely journey to seek help—as in the case of Joseph and Dion. But on every journey the first steps must be taken, however clumsy they may be.

Yet, the fact remains that the process of moving from pain to growth can be much too difficult in isolation. Reciprocal empathy is often necessary for enduring pain and using it creatively. Phillips and Taylor remark that, "Compassion and altruism have never found their place as significant terms in modern psychologies. And the apparent realism of self-interest stories . . . has made the kindness stories sound soppy and wishful" (Phillips & Taylor, 2009, p. 54). But then, there is a time for joy and a time for sorrow. When sorrow is unbearable, it damages the self and inclines us to mental illness; the empathic people are those who help in the time of sorrow with "just" some kindness. In fact, how much help do we need to survive? Perhaps not very much. It is perhaps no metaphor to say that severe pain breaks the heart, that it devastates our inner world, and yet, the "mere" kindness of people with a special talent for empathy is what often makes it endurable, and ultimately gets us across the abyss. Kohut, for one, makes the important point that healing is less dependent upon the theoretical position espoused by the therapist then the latter probably imagines. That is, provided that the psychoanalyst can, in fact, understand his patient sufficiently well and convey this understanding to the patient, healing will continue to occur, irrespective of the psychoanalyst's preference for, say, the Kleinian theory rather than a Freudian or Jungian perspective (Storr, 1997, p. 151). Wright, for instance, writes that a patient often taxed him to the extreme; it was primarily the fact that she experienced all of his interpretations as a form of control that threatened her very existence. Having tried every way of interpreting to no avail, Wright felt that any improvement in their relationship would be more therapeutic than the unremitting repetition and destructiveness that characterised the sessions (Wright, 2009, pp. 5–6).

Time and again, we see promising work met by a barrier of should-have-dones, could-have-dones, instead of being utilised as it is. It takes empathic support to overcome these situations. We may seek our well-known "mutative interpretations" to move us along from suffering to growth. This is the constant work that goes on in the most diversified forms of transference–countertransference vicissitudes of analytic settings. But then, we also think that this sort of work goes on in non-analytic settings, wherever there are efforts to educate and develop, to enhance whatever potential is in each one of us. The majority of psychoanalysts and other members of the so-called helping professions consider that intimate personal relationships are the chief sources of human happiness. Conversely, it is widely assumed that those who do not enjoy the satisfactions provided by such relations are neurotic or immature, or, in some other way, abnormal. But what is the reason for this assumption? Today, the thrust of most forms of psychotherapy is directed towards understanding what has gone wrong with the patient's relationships with significant persons in the past, so that the patient can be helped towards making more fruitful and fulfilling human relationships in the future (Storr, 1997, pp. 5–6). Fruitful? Helpful? For what? Probably for moving from pain to growth. Relations are the indispensable ingredient, or catalyst, of the forward movement from suffering to development. The lack of sufficiently empathic relations lets us become deadened with indifference and overwhelmed by the only news that we can receive—the bad news. If we are left alone while trying to metamorphose pain into growth, we might not succeed eventually, and thus might lapse into a "painless" form of dullness: the invisible threat of benumbment. This is, perhaps, the hidden reason for our current inclination to praise relationships more than anything else.

Of course, we need a modicum of empathy to use pain creatively, but it is not easy to obtain or offer empathy for growth while the experience of suffering is seen as something that has to be carefully concealed. Yet, if we are not sufficiently aided by some interpersonal empathy, we cannot brave inner pain and somehow transmute it into an enhancing experience. (In fact, significantly, it just so happened that Joseph and Dion travelled together.) We risk being trapped into a vicious circle that needs to be broken. Where? Anywhere, wherever we can make a breakthrough. Hesse's story is perhaps an edifying example of the necessity to overcome our fixity of roles, identities, and labels that can impede our forward movement. We can, in fact, creatively think of wounded healers, compassionate fighters, authoritative servants, etc. The question is, how can we possibly connect the fixed nature of roles, as a form of dulling anaesthetic, to the quest for maturation? Abandoning rigidity of roles is a first step, and a very disruptive one, in our laborious journey to maturity. But then, adhesion to a role hounds us everywhere as a very tempting solution, the first quick-fix analgesic solution in our human venture. Paradoxically, it takes professional integrity and a firm identity to consciously opt for a reversal of roles. After all, am I not the parent, the psychoanalyst, the appointed judge? As analysts, we know very well that colleagues are there to help and supervise if we are humble/brave enough to ask for that. Also, we could invoke the idea of a potentially deadening, interlocking stalemate between "masters" and "slaves", mothers and babies, healers and sufferers: Joseph and Dion somehow were able to overcome any fixity of roles. Not surprisingly, the most poisonous playmates for us in recovering creativity are people whose resources remain blocked by the fixity of identities. Our recovery threatens them. Our blocked "friends" might want us to stay blocked.

Remaining paralysed in whatever role can function as an effective psychic anaesthetic. For the sake of example, the interlocking contraposition between allies and enemies seems almost to anaesthetise us against the unthinkable pain of death. Of course, we easily identify with our heroes and are easily flooded with sympathy when they fall. An anaesthetising fixity of roles could be detected in the drastic opposition between damaging villains and good heroes, as we know exactly with whom we will identify. And, of course, we can all experience satisfaction when "our" villains fall, almost as if the fall of a villain could be a true relief, totally painless and indifferent. I think I remember sufficiently well an inscription that appears in the chapel of a famous university, an inscription that probably derives from a laborious process: ultimately, a transition from instant sympathy to hard-won empathy. The inscription says something like: *Harvardiana mater oblita non est filiorum suorum qui diversis sub signis pro patria ceciderunt*. (Roughly, "The great mother Harvard has not forgotten to mourn for those of her sons who lost their lives for their country under different flags".) A short list of typically German names follows the inscription. This is perhaps a step away from collective, tribal narcissism toward a more mature and responsible way of suffering. This labour is spared those who are content with sympathy, and wish to relax in it, those who do not struggle towards empathy. This creative level of psychic pain surpasses the grief deriving from forms of mere sympathy, that is, sharing pain with those more like us; it reaches out towards a form of suffering rooted in empathy, that is, the capacity to share pain even with those who are/feel quite different from us.

Of course, we privilege the "strong" kindness of empathy over the "weak" kindness of sympathy (Corradi Fiumara, 2009, pp. 54–112). As we know, while sympathy is a natural inclination, empathy is a creative venture. It is a way of knowing and being known that almost exceeds our capacities. Roughly, sympathy can be seen as the inclination for very short psychic moves that might not go beyond our narcissistic territory; empathy is a propensity for more extensive moves that reach the difference-bearing features of others. But why do not ethnocentric narcissists ever try to be empathic? They probably just cannot. Joseph and Dion were very different from one another, but mature enough to prefer empathy to sympathy. Again, we are led back to the paradox that feeling comfortable can be a very poor measure of the creative quality of life. With all the contradictions of life, when we manage to endure suffering in a creative way, it is still the better alternative to the dullness of uncreative struggle. Not only this: what we avoid in ourselves, we tend to load on to our neighbours. What we carry consciously for ourselves frees the other from an imposed burden/role. Thus, there is no greater love than accepting our psychic pain and sparing our partners the burden of carrying it in our stead. In fact, it is only for the sake of illustration that we invoke relational vicissitudes such as those between mothers and babies (Winnicott), lords and bondsmen (Hegel), or healers and sufferers (Hesse). Of course, there can be innumerable co-existential situations requiring more lively and less static interaction. Almost as if a general pursuit of inner life and forward motion might be hard to eliminate in whatever human community, or dyad, even though we can go about this pursuit in a variety of ways.

Company and *solitude*

"Although suffering may come from our body, or from the external world, it primarily comes from our relations to other men." In Freud's view, "The suffering which comes from this last source is perhaps more painful to us than any other" (Freud, 1930a, p. 77). Conversely, perhaps, the gratification and the redeeming compensation that we can derive from others is also stronger than any other.

> Against the suffering which may come upon one from human relationships the readiest safeguard is voluntary isolation, keeping oneself aloof from other people. The happiness which can be achieved along this path is, as we see, the happiness of quietness. (Freud, 1930a, p. 77)

Is it a question of mere quietness, or of paralysis, repetition, and blockage? And then, how can we provide for ourselves the inner right to deserve approval? Here, Freud seems to approach the central human question of company *and* solitude. I shall try to elaborate on this point with the hypothesis that we ultimately seek a greater freedom in moving from one to the other focus; we wish to create a two-way circulation between our need for company *and* a need for solitude. Our human suffering, in fact, seems profoundly interwoven with these options and unending fluctuations. As I have said, our present preoccupation with relationships has replaced former anxieties about the unpredictability and precariousness of the natural world. In modern, affluent societies, most of us are protected from disease, hunger, and natural catastrophes to an unprecedented extent (Storr, 1997, p. 1). As Gellner puts it, "Our environment is now made up basically of relationships with others", and he goes on to affirm that the realm of personal relations has become "the area of our most pressing concern" (Gellner, 1990, quoted in Storr, 1997, p. 1). In fact, we have come to regard the cohesive company of others as the centre of higher forces sustaining mental life, and the experience of its overwhelming power is even thought to dissolve the negativity of solitude. But then, all human beings need uniquely personal interests as much as they need relationships; we are all geared toward the interpersonal as well as toward the uniquely personal. In Storr's view, the happier lives are probably those in which neither intersubjective relations nor very subjective interests are idealised as the *only* way to "salvation". An overemphasis on relations might impede the creativity that can develop if we can *also* endure an experience (or even a life) of solitude. If "relation" is the buzzword these days, the all-pervasive slogan, we could become obsessed with company and come to loathe solitude as much as we abhor inner pain. At the extreme, if I cannot bear to be alone, I might simply go along with any perverse relation, or any collective folly. According to Storr, "The capacity to be alone thus becomes linked with self-discovery and self-realization; with becoming aware of one's deepest needs, feelings and impulses" (Storr, 1997, p. 21).

From this perspective, then, some individuals are psychically "rich" while others are somehow "poor". As we know, psychoanalysis is primarily concerned with letting the individual be in touch with his deeper feelings. The setting could be described as allowing the individual to be alone—even in the presence of the analyst. The famous use of the couch not only encourages relaxation–regression, but also avoids eye contact between analyst and analysand. This is intended to safeguard the patient from being too preoccupied with the reactions of the analyst, and, thus, to enhance concentration on his own inner world. If we cannot bear solitude, that is, if we cannot endure the challenge of being alone (not "lonely" or "lonesome", just alone), we cannot ultimately afford to be spontaneous and creative. Similarly, if we cannot manage to find and engage with empathic allies to succeed in overcoming our fear of psychic pain, our fear of loss, we might remain confined in our fixed roles, our repetitive comfort zone. As we shall see, our fear of loss is ultimately more compelling than our desire to gain.

If we could be trained to tolerate the pain of loss, our daily negotiations would probably become more convenient. For the sake of illustration, we could note that an academic title obtained from some prestigious institution may work as an effective anaesthetic against the pain of confronting losses, especially losses of self-esteem. We wonder whether psychoanalysis, or friendship, or experience could empower us to overcome the paralysing painfulness of loss. In other words, one could not possibly lose prestige in highly regarded company if there is some written proof of one's worth from some prestigious institution. Our deeper self probably strives to gain the sort of personal authority that is not dependent on the approval of others, yet we crave the acceptance of our peers as if it were life itself, and a considerable amount of energy is expended on this venture. Thus, we have to hide everything about ourselves that others might not find laudable. Paradoxically, the hiding place might become our own most cherished part of the self—the locus of survival. If we could manage to reconnect to it on friendly terms, we might no longer be afflicted by the torment of what the audience might think; we could perhaps express ourselves with a spontaneity we have never known before. The re-conjunction of the self and its so-called shadow does not generate some doubled structure, in terms of an addition of one part to another. Rather, it generates a more complex structure in the sense of something ulterior, something richer than one plus one. The increasing acceptance of our "shadow" confers a force (not power, force) that does not come from the approval of anyone outside you; it is the authority you can access only when you are speaking from that innermost part of the self that can embrace its very shameful shadow.

What we conceal for fear of becoming unpopular, and thus condemned to solitude, may even take the form of unconscious guilt. Of course, it can be extremely laborious to deal with one's own guilt (even if it were the absurd guilt of trying to survive and be creative). If we resort instead to experiences of "corporate" guilt, we may conceal and/or avoid the danger of languishing in solitude; we can eschew contacts with our shadow, but also sever links with any creative potential. The hidden part of the self that no one should perceive, in case it leads to solitude, can be loaded on forms of collective, corporate guilt/shame. And so, opportunely, we can count on company to dilute it. One could then insist on being guilty only in respect of belonging to hypothetical classes of offenders, such as, for instance, the class of westerners, males, capitalists, etc. We can feel ourselves to be part of an iniquitous social group and to share a corporate guilt, or try to project it entirely into different corporations. This can be true, but it is also a hindering identification that exploits forces and truths for our own deception. According to Lewis, we should beware lest we are habitually making use of corporate guilt to distract our attention from old-fashioned guilt of one's own, which has nothing to do with any systems and which can be confronted without waiting for epochal changes (Lewis, 2012, p. 54). By "corporate" guilt, Lewis probably means a *collective* sense of guilt related to our social habitat; we may be guilty of exploiting women for work, children for projections, and the Third World for natural resources. But then, after all, doesn't everyone do that? We could *generically* be guilty of exploiting the southern hemisphere for resources, and yet continue tranquilly to sell "English" tea, "Swiss" chocolate, or "Italian" coffee, as if a plant of tea, cocoa, or coffee had ever grown in the northern hemisphere. Personal guilt is not fashionable; it is too painful, for one thing. But then, if we do not snare our unpresentable, shadowy part of the self, we cannot easily move between company and solitude. For corporate guilt and projected guilt cannot be handled with the same force as personal guilt. For most of us, as we are now, corporate guilt is a mere excuse for evading the real issue. Whether we share communal guilt, or project it on to other communities, we become anaesthetised to genuine remorse and, thus, free from the burden of confronting our individual failures.

We can, of course, think of ulterior, different ways to exorcise our fear of solitude. One is the common fascination with romantic love.

Precipitating one into intimate, satisfying company, falling in love is one of the solutions. Falling in love is, for the majority of us, one of the most compelling emotional experiences that anyone can encounter. According to Storr, while the state of being in love persists, the person engaged in it usually feels an irresistible sense of unity both with the outside world and also with the self (Storr, 1997, p. 186). This sense of unity that is initiated by recognising the beloved person might continue to exist even in the absence of his or her physical presence. Being in love is usually considered as the closest, most intimate form of relationship. But then, as stated earlier, all human beings need personal interests as well as very intense relations; we are all geared towards the interpersonal as well as to the uniquely personal (Storr, 1997, pp. 201–202). Not only the events of early childhood, but a host of other factors may influence whether individuals turn predominately to intersubjective relations or towards creative solitude to find the affective focus of their lives. When neither interpersonal relations nor uniquely personal interests are idealised as the only way to salvation, we can probably use our human suffering to the full (Storr, 1997, p. 201). We cannot say that company is incomparably better than solitude and that we are facing an either/or dilemma. In our encompassing perspective on human suffering, we try to argue that we need to create a two-way circulation of currents between company and solitude, as a condition for the spontaneous use of both.

The wish to gain and loss aversion

The title of this chapter, "The relational outlook", is intended to indicate that our creative use of inner pain is so very challenging that we actually need relations (in the form of solidarity, group support, and empathy) to sustain our forward movement. The idea of support, especially, applies to our constant critical condition of having to deal with a strong loss aversion that threatens to prevail over our desire for gain. Patients do not only cry or express feelings in a vacuum, they do so in our presence, and it is, thus, a here-and-now-exploration that allows for the use of the therapeutic encounter (Yalom, 2011, pp. 71–72). In analysis, we live through an alternating sequence of evocations and actual experiences followed by a joint work of integration of affects—especially the stormy, painful affects representing our dreadful fear of loss. A dual situation of company is, thus, necessary in our confrontation with the fear of loss. Anyone engaged in a maturational journey is propelled by a desire to gain (spontaneity, intimacy, success) but is even more paralysed by the ever-present fear of loss (of identity, status, comfort). Thus, we complain about this constant fear that sometimes seems to prevail over our wish for gain. Baggini, for instance, remarks that complaint is doubly transitive, in the sense that you do not only complain *about* something, but you also complain *to* someone, as if the interlocutor is necessary to allow us to express complaint (Baggini, 2010, p. 2). A hypothetical condition of isolation would not even allow us to alleviate suffering through complaint, through the expression of our refusal to accept that things are not as they should be. Ultimately, we complain that too little may be gained in comparison to what might be lost. Baggini reminds us of the familiar scenario in which someone appears to be having a moan and is told to stop complaining: I am not complaining, comes the reply, I am just saying (Baggini, 2010, p. 2): saying for the sake of seeing, through a joint perspective, that which we wish to gain as well as our gripping fear of loss. But then, if we could for a moment reverse our logic, surpass our psychic condition, it is the idea of losing, of failing, that gives definition, intensity, and perhaps meaning to the desire for winning and gaining. It would be futile just to achieve gains repeatedly. We usually have sufficient knowledge/experience of the emotions that accompany our sense of unearned good fortune. What we may truly want is the capacity to earn, and be the active cause of, our fulfilment. As long as we can only receive, or do no more than collect gains, we may remain secretly unhappy. We seem to be saying to our sufficiently good parents, "Thank you, that is good enough, thank you, but what I would really like is to overcome my fears of loss and finally offer, share, and produce some love of my own." We seek times and spaces in which to experiment with our capacity to radiate and bestow. If we did not confront our fears of loss, perhaps we could not be truly creative, be producers of love and nutrients. If we were entirely free from the infesting fears of loss, perhaps we could not experiment with the exercise of giving some outgoing love and generosity. One might be nauseated by constant gaining or receiving. But then, there are also losses that barely disguise gains, and for the use of these gains (for the purpose of eventually feeling like adult givers), we might, perhaps, brutally ask in what way a painful loss can serve us, or where it might direct our efforts. The scriptures say that God is the giver of everything, but could we perhaps do something comparable? Yet, while stubbornly trying to become producers and givers of life-enhancing forces, we might still feel the need to protect our inner world from extraction by others, in as much as others may still be perceived as posing a threat.

From a broader, co-existential perspective of potential reciprocities, we could say that our friendships are relations in time and space where our capacity for life is nourished by means of presence and fidelity throughout changes. If we can discover new wavelengths of presence, then we can find our own indispensable nutrients. A friend is one who can see our shadow and then be a mirror for so much *more* than our shadowy parts. It means embracing the mad and the sane in the other person. But the sort of empathy (not sympathy) that can even embrace shadows requires a slow, laborious cultivation over the years in order to blossom eventually; this is the real measure of our adventures in gaining and losing with our friends. Empathy is indeed costly and demanding; it cannot be extorted or stolen. A mature patient who also worked in her youth as an "escort", calling on her clients at home, complained bitterly about her former profession. What was unbearable for her was being asked to "stay a little longer", listen to stories of affliction, and help *not to fear* a wide range of possible losses. This made her feel exhausted and emptied, almost as if a sexual encounter could entitle the client to some fusional contact that would allow him to pour out the fears of loss that paralysed his wish to gain. But, of course, the empathy that is (reciprocally) needed in cultivating a friendship is intended to surmount any pervading fear of loss and become free enough to explore opportunities for gain. We often seek shortcuts and pre-emptive remedies to allay our fears of loss. As I have said, because of our fear of losing respect and prestige, we become desperately keen upon official (academic) documents confirming our worth—intellectual and cultural.

Once again, empathic company, like friendship, can only flourish if it does not turn into a fusional relation. Paradoxically, we can make good use of company to the extent that we can also afford to be alone. When we look inside ourselves and we catch glimpses of our shadow, we become ashamed. Our immediate reaction is to turn away, to turn our gaze away from ourselves in search of some tangible, external evidence of our worth. This often takes the form of looking to others for approval and validation, almost to the point of extorting it. The world's advertising industry uses fantastic amounts of resources to prey upon our pervasive need for social acceptance. One of the many tangible expressions of this need can be found in a burning desire for ourselves and for our offspring to become validated by some prestigious institution. If you do not, you can be stuck alone with your shadow and in consequent solitude. As if we could acquire a psychic *locus* in which to silently proclaim, "How can you possibly think that I am not wonderful when, in fact, I graduated from such a wonderful institution?" The qualities of teaching, resources, or networking are perhaps less relevant when compared to the power they convey for us to ignore our shadow on account of a superior endorsement, almost as if an oracle proclaimed our desirability. (What could I possibly gain from "Mole College" or "Tentative University?"). This secret power is worthy of any effort and expenditure. Even the most serious and notable institutions seem secretly to promise some ultimate treasure, and the young will want to pay any price to be accepted by a place where they can be sure to find it. This "treasure" can function as an amulet (a fetish) against fear of loss, something that will allow them tranquilly to seek gains. Conversely, and delusionally, we might even come to undervalue Shakespeare or Dostoevski just because the book is approached in some "minor" place of learning.

If we would look at our everyday life in a world of never-ending negotiations that extend from business to family life, Kahneman can definitely enlighten us (Kahneman, 2011, p. 305). To put it in its extreme form, human beings fight harder to prevent losses than to achieve gains. Losses are just *too* painful. Negotiators often pretend intense attachment to some asset (or condition), although they actually consider that "good" as a bargaining chip and intend to give it away in an exchange. Because negotiations are sustained by an idea of reciprocity, a concession that is presented as painful calls for an equally painful (and perhaps equally inauthentic) concession from the other side and, thus, a potential gain. It is said that management advisers often encourage employees to be daring and take initiatives. But then, most of us, and especially employees, tend to be risk averse. Dobelli reminds us that this aversion makes perfect sense (Dobelli, 2013, p. 102).

Why take risks that bring only minor gains? The downside carries much more weight than the upside: what happens in case of loss?

Safeguarding one's career strongly prevails over any potential reward. If employees do take big risks, it is often when they can hide behind group decisions. Risks always look too big, and loss is so fearsome. On the other hand, there is virtually no fear of risk and pain when we can, so to speak, go to war *all together*. Ultimately, it seems that fear of evil is more compelling than any wish for some good. We are more sensitive to the negative than to the positive motivations, and, thus, we gather into cohesive groups that alleviate our painful fear of loss. As is generally known, we remember bad behaviour longer than we remember good conduct, except, of course, when it comes to ourselves (Dobelli, 2013, p. 102). The idea of loss aversion (avoidance of pain at any cost) is an ever-present feature of negotiations. In Kahneman's view, existing terms define reference points, and a proposed change in any respect of the agreement is inevitably viewed as a concession that one side makes to the other (Kahneman, 2011, p. 304). Loss aversion creates a motivational asymmetry that makes agreements difficult to reach. The concessions that you make to me are my gains, but are your losses; they cause you much more pain than they give me pleasure. Inevitably, you will place a higher value on them than I do. And Kahneman insists,

> The same is true, of course, of the very painful concessions you demand from me, which you do not appear to value sufficiently. Negotiations over a shrinking pie are especially difficult, because they require an allocation of losses. People tend to be much more easygoing when they bargain over an expanding pie. (Kahneman, 2011, p. 304)

This is something we only know too well: in psychic distress, our pie is in a process of fearsome reduction. We are, thus, more terrorised by loss than we can be attracted by any gain that solitude might offer. And so we come to think that sustaining company is absolutely necessary in these confrontations and that we could not possibly survive in solitude.

CHAPTER SIX

The question of endurance

Nirmala: patiently resisting non-existence

Nirmala was not a beauty: slightly protruding teeth, low stature, heavy bottom, and difficult skin. Her speech was never clear either in English or in Italian, for it was mostly limited, broken language. This did not diminish the effect of her radiant smile and of her obstinate efforts to struggle on. This is how she came to me.

At that time there was a wealthy lady who had three children and who had made arrangements for a highly qualified English nanny to come to stay with her. However, the qualified nanny never arrived and so she was desperately trying to find a temporary solution. A neighbour spoke to her of a girl, a "poor creature" who was looking for any kind of job; she could hardly make herself understood, but seemed warm-hearted, good natured, and had the proper immigration papers. Perhaps, for a few days, she would do, and so the lady could continue going to work as the manager of restaurants. Nirmala was given a small room and a bathroom that she kept as clean as possible to make a good impression. The children in the family, aged three, five, and seven, immediately liked her as if she was some kind of very interesting creature, and competed in making fun of her way of speaking. But they did genuinely like her, became very attached to her, and made life enjoyable for her in the family. She had little competence in housework and, in just a few weeks, she damaged quite a few pieces of home equipment. She cooked fairly well and always did her best with what was bought. At the same time, talk about a qualified English nanny infuriated the children, who declared that they wanted Nirmala to stay. Broken language, household breakages, and requests for assurance that there were no evil ghosts in the apartment made the employer decide that Nirmala was both handicapped and insane. She then spoke to the neighbour who had introduced Nirmala and said she could not cope with that sort of girl. The neighbour said that there was "some sort of psychologist" in the neighbourhood and suggested that she refer Nirmala to me with the request to fix her as quickly as possible; otherwise, obviously, she could not keep such an impossible kind of girl.

And so Nirmala, from India, came and told me her story. She explained to me that a religious organisation made her join a group of girls who were about to fly to Rome, and also provided her with regular immigration papers. She told me that she was the fourth child in the family, and that from the very beginning she was told that she was definitely ugly, and that she could only babble instead of speaking. She was told that she was a house pet, and a useless one. She was considered so worthless that no good clothes or schooling were provided for her: she barely learnt to read and write from her older brothers and sister. She was sent to a part-time school where they taught her to sew, to darn and to patch clothes. Once, she also told me with bitterness that she was the darkest in the family. In every respect she was someone to get rid of and was constantly told that it would have been much better if she had not been born at all. The ridicule about her speech seeped into her inner world and made her feel hopelessly worthless. She was told that sometimes special, invisible ghosts take away the burden of such children from their families. And yet her older sister also told her that she was lovely, and her older brothers did not permit her to be unjustly beaten. Her sewing teacher frequently complimented her on her proficiency and interest in the subject.

Shortly before she was put on the aeroplane to Rome, her parents had made "arrangements" with a very poor widow whose son, Sati, was about to embark as a merchant seaman on a three-year contract.

If Sati would be prepared to propose to Nirmala, they would give the family an advance payment on a generous dowry (which did not exist, and which they had no intention of paying). In order to leave some money with his poor mother, the boy was virtually forced to propose to Nirmala, and then he disappeared to fulfil his seagoing contract. He had reluctantly accepted the deal, which would only be concluded in some distant future after his contract ended. The boy's relatives were very happy with this business opportunity. The non-payment of the promised dowry, however, was enough to invalidate any agreements. The widowed mother of the boy had practically forced her son to accept the engagement in order to secure a small advance on the dowry, a great deal of money that would never materialise. It was a fraud, and Nirmala's parents were well aware of possible retaliations. The advance payment was essentially a move to get rid of her. In the course of treatment, Nirmala told me with terror that when there were problems with a dowry not paid as promised, the husband might feel entitled to get rid of the bride in any way without being prosecuted.

The cost of therapy absorbed a great part of her earnings and she did extra work to compensate for this; she came between 2 and 4 p.m. when, by law in Italy, house workers are entitled to rest. When the sick mother of her employer came to stay with the family, she also took care of her with devotion and good grace, taking her out for walks after having put bright red lipstick on her.

This is an approximate chronicle of the events. But what went on and developed inside Nirmala? She recalled her childhood as a prison from which she could not escape while also being told that she should not exist. But the whole idea of escape merely reinforced her sense of helpless imprisonment because a little girl, unlike an adult, is someone who cannot choose to leave. But then this fantasy was also frightening, because she could not know what lay ahead. And if the present hurt so badly, she always saw the future as an even worse impending pain. It felt unreal that she had been made to become "engaged" *and* that she could suddenly board an aeroplane and go far away. She liked Sati because he used to live in the neighbourhood and somehow she knew him, while he had never noticed Nirmala. What was impressive about Nirmala was her constant, tacit knowing, in the sense that she knew much more than she was able to tell. She was unable to put into words how she accomplished her deep and accurate knowledge. Her true knowledge lay in her ability to use it. She had never heard of analysis, for instance, but she decided for it, submitted to it. The idea of being thrown out of the house was just too terrifying.

Nirmala was astonished to see and touch the bright, wonderful clothes of the seven-year-old girl in the family, a very shy little girl. She was truly struck with admiration. Like any lightning rod, she received the lightning only because she was its privileged receptor. Sensitive to these kinds of images, she perceived the girl better than others did and was hoping for the best for her, affectionately encouraging her to wear her beautiful dresses and enjoy the experience: another traumatised person might have felt hatred or envy. A part of her personality had been shaped by events that became imprinted in her psyche, and made her exceptionally sensitive to this sort of beauty. Her ideal self, her aspirations and daydreams, revealed what could still make her quite lively, although she had known both spoken and unspoken injunctions not to be alive, to simply not exist. This was the sort of pain that was beyond any expression and almost unthinkable: she became familiar with it by comparing it with occasional, rare encouragements to grow and live, the same kind of encouragement she gave to the little girl. Although it had not been her own experience, she was happy to realise that such encouragement functioned well and elicited responses.

Encouragement for what? For her own life? Nirmala could not tell me about projects, goals, or aspirations. Perhaps she could not find the words or concepts to engage me in this sort of talk. As we patiently shared her inner vicissitudes, it became clear that, for her survival purposes, the journey itself was the point of arrival. There was no final destination. She wanted to grow because she could not endure the horror of being considered inadequate, losing her job, and relapsing into non-existence, away from everything. Her destination was her daily struggling with creativity and she was very much attached to it. She was an authentic, ordinary genius. She played along in the time she had and this play encompassed, for her, the mystery of joy. In her early years there was no mercy for her afflictions: she learnt that she could not even afford to be unhappy, that she could get no attention or reassurance with regard to her crippling fears—such as evil ghosts removing unwanted children from their families. Nirmala had actively engaged me in fighting non-existence with her. She could not theorise it; she only wanted help in her fight against horror—however invisible, intangible, or ineffable. She wanted to learn to move from moment to moment because she had no opportunities for long-term projects, career, or success.

Her father and his acolytes had been prisoners of his grandiose contempt for other people, making the house a mad enclave against the world; his will was law and his mood constituted the family's daily weather. Her mother was an extrapolation of her father and was often seeking pardon for giving birth to a creature such as Nirmala: unacceptable, shameful, a house pet at best. Talk of her disgraceful birth was always around and no one objected to it. I frequently wondered how she had survived. Nirmala tried to combat this condition with a sense of quality in what she did—even the most simple, small action or remark, darning clothes, thanking the teacher. Our sessions were all about minimal details, appreciation of feelings, microscopic events of which she could be a protagonist. She resisted non-existence and attached herself to the tiniest links. Analysis was all about tiny inner movements that could be recognised and appreciated. There developed an increasing sense of quality in what she did, both inwardly and outwardly. Quality increasingly implied the care and attention that come with awareness. These were our first steps. This does not mean we knew where we were going; it just means that these steps were primary and the destination quite secondary (and she had no conception of destinations). In analysis, she started to give herself permission to begin small and proceed in baby steps. She feared like the plague setting ideal goals, for those goals created unbearable fears, which induced procrastination and the self-accusation of being lazy. She was content to respond to the present. Her special talent was in the activities of daily life and her interactions with others—as though just "being": call it survival, growth, development, or whatever. For years and years, for instance, she sent birthday greetings and Christmas cards to her "fiancé" and she never had a reply.

Many things happened in the course of ten years of analysis. Nirmala had become a superb cook, with a whole library of cookery books and sophisticated instruments. She even received professional requests from restaurants. After a complicated sequence of employment shuffles, Sati finally arrived in Rome, working as a driver for an American businessman. There was going to be a function sponsored by the Indian embassy in a large theatre. In the weeks that preceded the event, she prepared for it as best as she could. Her employer let her borrow a magnificent sari that she had bought in India, as well as her own jewellery. Nirmala had very high heels, an impressive hairstyle, and impeccable make-up. When she saw Sati at the function, she waved and smiled at him, but he did not respond and immediately looked in another direction. She felt like dying. "But then, I have been well trained in dying all the time", she told me. Nevertheless, she went closer to Sati and greeted him once again. He said, "Oh, I am terribly sorry, I did not recognise you. You are such a beauty!" She was married in India with a very special celebration: an agency provided her with photography, dresses, jewellery, hairstyling, make-up, shoes, and everything else she needed. Upon returning to Rome, Sati and Nirmala shared her single bed at her employer's home. Nirmala would finally have a baby of her own at the age of forty-three.

The less travelled path

"We cannot help but feel deeply *grateful* for the descriptions of human anguish", remarks Davies (2012, p. 145). The injunction not to exist can be a serious source of anguish. We need, in fact, to become more familiar with the multiformity of inner pain to regard it as constitutive of human life, and, thus, try to free ourselves from a collective imposition to be happy, or to at least try to *appear* successful and satisfied. But, here, we try to explore a less travelled path. We try to confront the variety of dejections with which so many of us are struggling—whether we are beggars or kings. Afflictions abound for everyone. It is paradoxical, moreover, that on top of suffering we should also be ashamed of our inner travail. As if in addition to feeling sad, we should also feel bad and mad. Nirmala had managed to escape this ulterior consequence. The underlying thesis here is that familiarity with the variegated vicissitudes of pain may also deliver us from the unnecessary and uncreative burden of being ashamed. As we know, shame is conducive to a collective, elusive inner paralysis—the very opposite of creative suffering. And, of course, inner adversity does not discriminate on the grounds of success; it is as likely to ensnare the man who lives quietly as the celebrated star of the moment.

It seems that *perforce* nowadays, we must return to Bion's question of the evasion of pain. In fact, the idea that all kinds of inner pain can be anaesthetised without serious consequences is probably an illusion.

In "A theory of thinking", Bion unequivocally remarks that, "A capacity for tolerating frustration enables the psyche to develop thought as a means by which the frustration that is tolerated is itself made more tolerable" (Bion, 1962, p. 306). This sounds like a very good deal, even though it feels like having to bear with inner paradoxes, going uphill, or swimming against the tide.

In Caper's synthetic *aperçu*, the loss of a loved object (person) precipitates unconscious hatred towards it, resulting in an internal struggle between one's love *and* hatred for the (same) object (Caper, 1999, p. 101). The labour (pain) of mourning is due to this struggle and to the remorse (literally, the backbite) that one feels as a result of hating a "receding" person that one also loves. Hatred might gain the upper hand at first, with the result that one's love for the lost object and one's capacity to love in general are temporarily compromised. What we refer to as working through loss is a process that has no clear ending and is, in fact, sustained by a cultivated familiarity with inner pain.

In a medieval, incisive description of our burden of living, we are offered a tentative presentation of our inner torments, a "description of human anguish" for which Davies might be grateful. A classical text suggests that, in our earthly experience,

> We mourn our bitterness and weariness, for the days of this life are short and evil, full of grief and pain. Here man is defiled by many sins, ensnared by many passions, a prey to countless fears. Racked by many cares, and distracted by many strange things, he is entangled in many vanities. He is hedged in by many errors, worn out by many labours, burdened by temptations, enervated by pleasures, tormented by want. (A'Kempis, 1952, p. 157)

A dramatic exaggeration? A terrifying medieval outlook? It could be, but perhaps also an enlightening challenge to our imposed masquerade of living successfully—almost in an atmosphere of "smile or die". In fact, we are trying a more difficult path as a way of becoming familiar with inner pain; familiarity may get us through it, perhaps. As has been mentioned previously, in the face of our afflictions we are all in search of quick remedies (or tricks): we seek the right ontology or the right psychology, the right mantra or right partner—whatever offers relief from an unbearable struggle. This desire for instant tricks, for "magical" solutions, reflects our wish for prompt transformations, for rescue and protection (Hollis, 2003, p. 75). It is a common complaint, even in psychoanalytic itineraries, that, after so much commitment, there should still be the labour of continuing effort. Here, again, we do not opt for "magic", but for the labour of coping with inner and outer reality. In adopting the perspective of the individual, rational person, we might even have to turn our face from the pervasiveness of rationality. For, in fact, we may easily abuse our free will and rationality, which is tantamount to seeking a trick to allow us to quit all our labours and ascend to the stars, or to some kind of paradise. As I said earlier, the trick (shortcut, device, theory) ranges from a metaphorical piece of fruit from a forbidden tree to an elaborate ideology. Conversely, if we can endure pain, we can opt for identification rather than imitation, we can opt for inner psychic actions rather than outer reactions—such as eliminating the different Laiuses mounted arrogantly on their chariots. Also, we should accept the discomfort of not knowing rather than consulting some sort of oracle as a shortcut to knowledge of our future. We could certainly exert ourselves to try to reach heaven rather than trying to break into it by using the simple means of a symbolic piece of fruit or a dose of a drug. Ultimately, the choices seem to be as simple as that. There can be all sorts of differences in our human condition, but also innumerable commonalities.

At the very outset of development, according to Winnicott, there is not really hatred but a primitive sort of love, that is, a ruthless demand that might even evoke a measure of resentment in the parent. The point, again, is that both partners must creatively endure this primitive sort of love—which might hurt as if it is hatred. Regarding the mother figure, Phillips writes, "Optimally, just like the analyst of the psychotic patient, she must not retaliate beyond the infant's capacity to make sense of her feelings. From the infant's point of view it can feel like a ruthless assault" (Phillips, 1988, p. 9). Furthermore, "The mother's depression is experienced by the child as an overriding demand that makes his own demands impossible" (Phillips, 1988, p. 92). We could consider the term "depression" as a generic, inclusive term indicating all sorts of fragilities or inadequacies. Thus, the child with a fragile, vulnerable mother figure can only live "reactively", to use a crucial Winnicottian concept. In fact, the child might have to endure the monotony of his psychic reactions and of not being capable of proper psychic actions. In Ferro's view, the first activity to set off the big bang that switches on the mind, in our species, is the massive evacuation of proto-sensorial, proto-emotional states by the child. If these evacuations (beta elements) are gathered, processed, and transformed by a mind that absorbs and metabolises them (alpha function), they are gradually converted into meaningful pictograms (Ferro, 2011, p. 69). This seems intuitive enough. Yet, the question remains, what happens if we cannot endure the pain caused by the proto-emotional world of the other? Therefore, this capacity to endure pain is the key element of all inner processes, both developmental and therapeutic.

Winnicott is also asking a simple question: given the infant's dependence on the mother, what may become of the child that makes up "successfully" for mothering deficits? This success enables the child to survive, but with the unconscious project and hope of subsequently finding an environment in which development could start up again. In Phillips' words, "A life could be lived, that is to say, in suspended animation" (Phillips, 1988, p. 93). But, again, also in this successful attitude, enormous patience and endurance are required. It can be difficult to tolerate the pervasive, suffocating pain, or sense of futility, born of necessary compliance in a stand-by position.

A synopsis of our current argument could be found in William James' enlightening remark:

> The method of averting one's attention from evil and living simply in the light of good is splendid as long as it will work. . . . Healthy mindedness [the act of focusing on only good and positive things] is inadequate as a philosophical doctrine, because the evil facts which it refuses positively to account for are a genuine portion of reality; . . . the only openness of our eyes to the deepest levels of truth. (James, 1985, quoted in Davies, 2012, p. 132)

And, "Failing to accord to sorrow . . . any positive and active attention whatever, is formally less complete than . . . trying at least to include these elements in our scope" (James, 1985, quoted in Davies, 2012, p. 133). Just "less complete", or gravely misleading?

As we know, when a relationship ends it can disrupt one's assumptions about who one is, about one's values, and what can be expected from others. If we do not become familiar with the work of re-evaluating all of our assumptions, and simply try to soldier on, or resort to powerful anaesthetics, we risk learning nothing from our troubles, and just perpetuating an abhorrence of inner pain. This attitude is accompanied by a particular kind of complaint, one that comes close to the medical sense of the word. In Baggini's view, "There is an acute sense that things should not have come to this, that there is something wrong with the world" (Baggini, 2010, p. 31). As if we were simply facing an objectionable disturbance of a physiological, silent way of functioning. When we must deal with problems, we instinctively resist trying the way that leads us through obscurity and darkness. We wish to hear only of unequivocal results, and tend to forget that these results can only be brought about when we have ventured into, and emerged from, the darkness. But then, can we endure darkness when confronting an invasion of beta elements (bizarre, threatening emotions)?

We cannot really say what brings us happiness. We can only pin down what blocks success and brings *un*happiness. And, thus, if we can simply eliminate the downside, the negative factors, the upside will presumably take care of itself. This is all we need to know—quite illusorily. But, in fact, we are all in the same boat, all trying to row through life. The psychologist Rolf Dobelli reports the case of a man dating three different women. He is in love with all three and can imagine starting a family with any (all?) of them. And yet, he simply does not have the heart to choose just one, because then he would be giving up the other two for good. It seems "smart" to refrain from deciding so that all options remain open, nothing is lost, and no pain is involved; no downside at all. But then, ultimately, no real relationship will ever develop. Options are not free of cost (Dobelli, 2013, pp. 304–305). They come at a price even though the price tag is often hidden or intangible. But then, the psychic action of paying a price for something confers a deeply felt sense of inner agency, *and* an escape from the secret torpor of passivity, however comforting and lucrative it may appear.

Of course, our smart ego tries to surmount difficulties by scheming, selecting, or acquiring appropriate anaesthetic remedies. Then, when we try to step away from our egoic strategies and try simply to live in the acceptance of what the case may be (of the "conditions that obtain", in Winnicott's language), there is less good or bad for us to applaud or fight (Corradi Fiumara, 2013, p. 44). There are only different options corresponding to our capacities to tolerate frustration. Thus, ultimately, we can be seriously stricken, but not "killed". Also, we are allowing offending people, the "Abels", as we might describe them, to be as they are. When the Abels are too offensive, the Cains feel entitled to retaliate. This capacity to permit others to exist as they are might take the Cains of our human brotherhood beyond the impulse to eliminate the "Abels" altogether.

Having endured situations of neglect and abuse, subjects may become imprisoned in the conviction that they are entitled to compensation for such unjust pains (Freud, 1916d, p. 312). In "The exceptions", Freud remarks that whenever analysts invite patients to make a provisional renunciation for the sake of a better, more creative prospect, or

> to submit to a necessity which applies to everyone, one comes upon individuals who resist such an appeal on a special ground. They say that they have renounced enough and suffered enough, and have a claim to be spared any further demands; they will submit no longer to any disagreeable necessity, for they are *exceptions* and, moreover, intend to remain so. (Freud, 1916d, p. 312)

He also points out that, of course,

> Their neuroses were connected with some experience of suffering to which they have been subjected in their earliest childhood, one in respect to which they knew themselves to be guiltless and which they could look upon as an unjust disadvantage imposed upon them. (Freud, 1916d, p. 313)

In Freud's view the exceptions are those who have gravely suffered, who have already paid the price for any occasion of pleasure, and, thus, have the right to exact or extort it. The word "exception" seems to imply a statistical outlook, indicating a deviance from the norm. But the problem is that, to varying degrees of severity, most of us may secretly believe that we truly *are* exceptions. As McDougall (1990) states, we are all "psychic survivors". In fact, pathology only amplifies an attitude that we all share to some extent. And failures, of course, only strengthen the perverse explanatory theory; as if we were saying, "Once again I am being cheated of that to which I have a right and I must, therefore, try even harder." There should, perhaps, be a better awareness of this widespread, elusive (unconscious?) problem, *and* empathy for this perverse, frustrating conviction/condition. Freud instructively paraphrases the words of Shakespeare's Richard III, lamenting his deformity: "I may do wrong myself, since wrong has been done to me" (Freud, 1916d, p. 315)—I am *entitled* to do so. Even an injudicious use and partial understanding of psychoanalytic literature could induce us to construct some "scientific" conviction of our victims' right to extort what we need. And it is perhaps worth recalling that not only individual subjects can suffer from this condition, but also entire communities or nations. We know this all too well from reading the most disparate historical events.

So, identification with a victim/hero model might prevent the individual from effectively dealing with an inner, thick tangle of painful threads—almost a tangible entity. The exceptional victims/heroes maintain that after all the harm that they have suffered from others, they are fully entitled to use their sorrowful identity as an inexhaustible asset. But they also keep themselves imprisoned in this coercive outlook. If one is still holding on to anger, resentment, or condemnation, one is firmly holding on to the inner tangle of painful strands, an almost inescapable tangle that keeps us in bondage to the past and annuls prospects. The tangle seems to have a consistency, almost a life, of its own that is constantly fighting to survive and expand; the exceptions tend to support it, Freud warns us. It almost functions as something that pretends to be the whole person. The sick tangle pretends to be who you are. It uses the person and his situation to get what it wants—easy gains or, paradoxically, even more pain.

This unfortunate inclination may be reinforced by the abuse or improper use of different psychological theories, in the sense that adverse conditions and traumas are utilised to "causally explain" the disruption of any personal agency. The logic is that once the disruption is "scientifically" accounted for, one may surreptitiously feel entitled to a total surrender to passivity, while also tranquilly entitled to exert all means to extort compensation. And that would solve the problem. How is that for a theory?

Travelling the path

Our exploration of creative suffering seems counter-intuitive and also seems to run against our evolutionary disposition to fear danger/pain and to avoid it at all costs. Yet, it is worth our while to take this path, even though with uncertain steps. Why uncertain steps? Because there are falls and wounds, regression and confusion to be suffered every few steps. Since we are naturally enabled to perceive potential pain more easily than we are to perceive libidinal opportunities, it is strange that culture should not provide us with remedial means for coping with the challenging experience of potential danger, pain, and loss (Kahneman, 2011, p. 301). We are so prone to perceiving signs of pain that we should wonder why the psychic side-effects of such an evolutionary blessing are not more explicitly investigated. We wonder why the edifying literature, which does not deny actual dangers, but teaches us to recognise and cope with them, is, in fact, so scarce. "Just smile and keep going" sounds like a grandiose and ultimately ineffective method of counselling. Natural threats are always there, but so are psychic, mental, and emotional threats, always painful. But then, we should start right from there as an initiatory alternative to hiding threatening occurrences. In an evolutionary outlook, people who were reckless or inattentive to threats died before they could pass on their genes to the next generation. Those who remained cautious survived, and we are their descendants. Thus, it is no wonder that we fear loss more than we value gain. Dobelli points out, for instance, that *losing* £100 costs us a greater amount of unhappiness than the delight you would feel if you *found* £100. Perhaps a loss weighs about twice as much as a comparable gain (Dobelli, 2013, p. 101). Social scientists call this attitude *loss aversion*. For this reason, if you want to convince someone about something, do not focus on the advantages; instead, highlight how it helps to avoid the disadvantages. Roughly, the fear of losing something is more compelling than the prospect of gaining something of equal value.

This discussion amounts to saying that avoidance of pain has a stronger motivational power than the desire for pleasure. What we seek, then, is familiarity with the stronger side of our motivation (fear of loss) for the sake of gaining a modicum of freedom *from* it, and, thus, the freedom to experience creative suffering and proactive psychic actions. If we could learn, re-learn, and learn again how to get away from a schizo-paranoid attitude in order to come through the struggles of the depressive position, we would certainly gain in terms of creativity and relatedness. Even psychoanalysis involves some endurance of pain for both partners in the dyad; so much so that Grotstein refers to it as a *"passion play* that seeks to externalize and thereby reveal a hidden conflict through dramatization (Grotstein, 2009, p. 258). He also says, "Passion designates both the suffering the patient is undergoing unconsciously and/or consciously, *and* the endeavour of the emotionally experienced containment capacity of the analyst" (Grotstein, 2009, p. 74). Unlike most psychoanalysts, past and present, he believes that psychoanalysis can be thought of as essentially constituting a "passion play", if we interpret "passion" as intense inner discomfort. "The frame", he suggests, "is the guardian of the analytic passion play" (Grotstein, 2009, p. 74). If we continued along the less travelled path by tentatively replacing the term "child" with "patient", and the term "parents" with "analysts", we could, perhaps, instructively read Winnicott saying that

> Patients must test over and over again their ability to remain good analysts in spite of anything patients may do to hurt them. They are good enough analysts to the extent that they can endure the pain, be consistently resilient, and not rejecting the patients. (Phillips, 1988, p. 67)

In Kleinian jargon, it is a question of abandoning the comfortable, exciting ways of projection for the sake of treading the provisionally less comfortable but more creative and relational path of enduring the paradoxes of a depressive outlook. Why is paradox involved? Because it is a question of recognising and holding together the contradiction of being both good *and* bad. While *formal* paradoxes violate only our logical stipulations, *psychic* paradoxes place endless strain on our own minds. Projection is an instant trick, a simple reaction, while the paradoxes involved in the depressive position involve a laborious itinerary and psychic action, in contrast to reaction. Through loving exploration and enhancing knowledge, we can gain familiarity with the discomfort of the less travelled path (a sort of *via negativa*), and, thus, forsake some illusory, all-positive homogeneity. Kierkegaard's irony can be enlightening on this point:

> One way is to suffer, another to become a professor of another's having suffered. The first is "the way"; the other is going roundabout (which is why the preposition "about" is like a motto for all instructing and instructional attitudes), and it may well end up going downabout. (Kierkegaard, 1996, p. 614)

The reactive, projective tricks ultimately amount to repetitive reactions (as if under a spell of repetition compulsion), while the toleration of our inner paradoxes allows for creative psychic actions, propelled by a search for truth, as Bion would say. In his view, "Whether true thoughts are entertained or not is of significance to the thinker but not to the truth. If entertained they are conducive to mental health; if not they initiate disturbance" (Bion, 1970, p. 116).

Bion also believes that "Physician and patient are alike in considering that the disease should be recognized by the physician; in psycho-analysis recognition must be by the sufferer too" (Bion, 1970, p. 6). In one of Doctor Johnson's letters quoted by Bion, we read,

> Whether to see life as it is will give us much consolation, I know not; but the consolation which is drawn from truth, if any there be, is solid and durable; that which may be derived from error must be, like its original, fallacious and fugitive. (Bion, 1970, p. 6)

This is a tentative synthesis of the laborious way to maturity, a way to be learnt, re-learnt, and learnt again. In Klein's words, "The infantile depressive position is the *central* position in the child's development. The normal development of the child and its capacity for love would seem to rest on how the ego works through this nodal position" (Klein, 1964, p. 310). To work through this nodal position we probably need "something more" that can give shape to our efforts to move forward. We might call it "interpretation", even though the form that gives shape to the experience is intrinsic to it. In Wright's opinion,

> The significance thus lies within the form itself, the same being true of significant movements—the moment comes, has its effect, and goes but it has no existence apart from the containing form. The same is true with the expression of pain. (Wright, 2009, p. 162)

If we could express in words what it meant, we would not be trembling or suffocating in our pain. Nirmala was told again and again that she should not have been born: "You'd better disappear" was the message. The therapeutic challenge consisted in trying to give some shape and form to her attempts to fight such a diffuse, deadening feeling. In Nirmala's case, her enforced belief that she should not exist functioned like an asphyxiating poison to be somehow countered and neutralised in therapy. The analytic work is about providing some psychic form for this sort of revolt, finding a way of pursuing a less travelled path and making it endurable.

In Ferro's view, communications of sorrow can only be accepted on the manifest level of pain, suffering, guilt, and anger. "But if we are in analysis there is more to it. In fact, to put the point radically so as to be absolutely clear: it is only this more that belongs specifically to us analysts" (Ferro, 2011, p. 20). Clear enough. This something more, however, has to become acceptable and usable. We should recall that symptoms and defences are the result of years of attempts to avoid a *worse* affliction; deconstructions and reconstructions in analysis are, thus, processes that must take into account the patient's threshold of tolerance to pain. Perhaps we need to remember constantly, with Bion, that "People exist who are so intolerant of pain . . . that they feel the pain but will not suffer it and so cannot be said to discover it" (Bion, 1970, p. 9). But then, once again, the crux of the problem is our relative tolerance/intolerance of pain. If this is so, why should we not pursue the most important of questions: how can we possibly develop this essential psychic capacity? It is essentially a capacity to move on, to keep going. How is that for a path?

Ferro reminds us that "The internal world is as real as the outside world and it is only the former that we as analysts are called upon (and competent) to deal with" (Ferro, 2011, p. 19). It is the internal world of two different persons, though. So, resisting the less travelled path is necessarily a joint venture, a dual effort to be constantly renegotiated with respect to the varying thresholds of pain. From Ferro's perspective, patients may even speak without knowing of their despair, pain, and losses. And yet, through the "something more" provided by different forms of containment, they can also understand "that this pain can likewise contain a gain, a development" (Ferro, 2011, p. 20).

When Nirmala could breathe more freely, as the poisonous introjects were gradually being detoxified, she became more capable of moving within external reality rather than just constantly avoiding its blows. She had come to therapy for fear of being considered insane, losing her job, and, thus, pushed back into a mortified, thing-like existence. She became able to grow plants, cook food, marry her fiancé, and have a son. It was the most profound joy when she realised that she had only to cook in a restaurant, and had no more cleaning to do.

In his sustained struggle to understand anxiety, Freud said that he was trying "To find something that will tell us what anxiety really is, some criterion that will enable us to distinguish true statements about it from false ones". And he continues, "Anxiety, then, is in the first place something that is *felt* . . . As a feeling, anxiety has a very marked character of un-pleasure . . . *of pain*" (Freud, 1926d, p. 132, my emphasis). The something more that is contributed by the analyst helps to impart liveable (viable) psychic form to this unpleasure, allowing movement away from its suffocating diffuseness. We can turn it into a liveable pain as an alternative to letting it proliferate as poisonous evil. It is a question of repossessing one's inner world rather than barely surviving its suffocating effects. The damaging affliction of inner torpor can be summarised in the words of Benjamin, especially where she points out that "An activity *without ownership* requires as its counterpart a perverse form of passivity" (Benjamin, 1990, p. 10). We all need help to repossess our mental life.

CHAPTER SEVEN

The challenge of interpretation

The use of metaphor

A theoretical framework, whether implicit or explicit in the formation of an analyst, may function both to reveal and to restrict our understanding of the clinical situation—it is, in fact, a *mode* of knowing. One set of meanings can be experienced as equivalent to psychic reality itself, while alternative meanings can be obscured by our frame of reference (Downing, 2000, p. 248). But then, from a psychoanalytic perspective, we are engaged in both approaching and developing ulterior inner realities; thus, we constantly engage in metaphorical efforts aimed at expanding our modes of knowing. Paradoxically, while a certain theoretical outlook, or primary metaphor, may represent a threat to the maturation of the analysand, therapeutic progress also depends on its very existence. Interpretative work primarily functions in this very real psychic contingency and, thus, results in a challenging confrontation. We face this challenge by means of constant metaphorical attempts to deepen and expand our knowledge. Our paradox is that a strong need to believe and a complementary need to question ourselves radically might be our best hope for retaining our creativity and integrity as analysts (Corradi Fiumara, 1995).

At the beginning of our western philosophical tradition, Aristotle clearly affirms that "The greatest thing, by far, is to be a master of metaphor. It is the one thing that cannot be learnt; and it is a sign of genius" (Aristotle, 1985, pp. 2234–2235). The "naturalist" philosopher insists that our metaphoric potential is "by far the greatest thing" in our relational language and an instrument for survival and creativity. In his words, "It is from metaphor that we can best get hold of something fresh" (Aristotle, 1985, p. 2239). Probably, "fresh" is intended to mean new, ulterior, deeper, original—which is what we seek in the challenge of interpretation. However, metaphors do not necessarily exhibit their metaphoricity on the surface, and what sounds like verbal imagery (free associations?) might turn out to be an embryonic hypothesis of how a question for which we lack words is to be posed. In fact, we strive to connect with something that we do not yet know. Although he does not employ the term "metaphor", Ferro suggests that in analysis links can become obvious and evident: "This means not only that they can be explained but also that the patient has the necessary tools to cope with the hardships that the vicissitudes of each bond imply" (Ferro, 2011, p. 105). The purpose of the analysis is to progressively add to the patient's set of tools that enable him to name, recontextualise, and metabolise emotions. "This is a psychoanalysis that is more concerned with tools for thinking than content" (Ferro, 2011, p. 105). It is a therapy addressed to empower the analysand to think and feel, for, in fact, contents can vary indefinitely.

Repeated attempts to tell one's life story not only constitute accounts, given in the here and now, of events that took place in the there and then. In the endeavour of recounting one's story, the narrator and the protagonist tend actually to coincide at the end of the story, an end that then functions as an inaugural opportunity for re-evaluating and reshaping underlying assumptions. Almost as if Robin Hood was finally told, "Dear Robin, you are not a thief; you are a libertarian and a revolutionist." This is an essential aspect of psychoanalytic work. At the "end" of the story, metaphoric links can be found indicating a few, or perhaps many, ways of going about life in a different way. For instance, deciding whether words are instruments or weapons, precious or worthless, whether the individual, or the group, *really* exists, whether danger comes from inside or from outside. As such primary connections become less obscure, the patient might also reveal the hitherto hidden guidelines in his development.

Ferro reminds us that Bion often says that there are already too many conceptual theories in psychoanalysis, and tries to provide us with a set of tools for thinking that we previously did not possess and which enable us to reflect on things we previously could not think (Ferro, 2011, p. 50). Our metaphoric potential is the prime psychic instrument for doing just that—for linking with the unknown. These tools are not only formal enrichments; they allow us to perform new operations or to acquire an awareness of the operations performed in the consulting room, an awareness that we previously did not have (Ferro, 2011, p. 50). Interpretation is a challenge because the bi-personal "here-and-now" constantly varies in complexity and intensity. Also, of course, the prospect of a challenge implies potential distress and defeat—psychic suffering, ultimately.

We are frequently tempted to remain uninformed, unchallenged, safe in a self-referential paradigm, imprisoned in a standard vocabulary, frozen by the lack of metaphoricity. "Ignorance, xenophobia, bigotry and stultification feed on self-referential jargons", in Hollis's words (Hollis, 2003, p. 87). There is nothing automatic, formal, or deductive about psychoanalytic interpretation: it amounts to a sequence of creative challenges that we confront by means of our personal metaphoricity. From this outlook, we can say with Ferro that

> The session becomes a shared, co-narrated, co-acted dream where stories, transformations, insights come to life—but also above all aptitudes to dream, to transform into reverie, into emotion, into image, into the ability to dream what has taken the pressing form of an abscess of sensoriality to which we have no access. (Ferro, 2011, p. 10)

But then, of course, there can be pre-existent lumps, obnoxious stories that we have to cope with. Ferro insists on the importance of weaving together *new* stories or dreams (Ferro, 2011, p. 10). This is all the more important if we consider that the sufferer may be sadly imprisoned in *old*, deadening stories that curtail his inner life. Although it is widely acknowledged that metaphors have a role to play in mental development, the question of whether this is generally formative or potentially impairing remains hardly explored. We can, thus, suspect the presence of obscured, anti-maturational features of metaphoric guidelines; these can introduce constraints and blind spots that are detrimental to psychic growth. Just think of Nirmala's family jargon, in which the metaphor of her being a "house pet of some kind" and of her "superfluous birth" constantly circulated.

Established metaphors can, in fact, introduce pre-emptive blocks. We must, therefore, generate ulterior, alternative metaphors. In fact, we use metaphors by participating in the vision that they suggest. Even when the vision is actually a cause of blindness, we may accept the damage for the sake of belonging, for the sake of preserving our own role in our micro- or macro-community. This is part of the challenge of psychoanalytic interpretation. The interpretation of a metaphor can be enforced so as to endorse the specific doings of the person(s) generating the metaphor or propagating a particular view of events, such as, for instance, "She is a pet animal". If a developing person becomes convinced of being utterly worthless, there is no cognitive input from reality that will change that person's personal outlook. Humans seem to develop at the earliest opportunity a complex view of reality, which they use to supplement what they know nothing about. When confronted with novel, disconcerting situations, we are tempted to produce an explanation that might account for the new data in terms of our innermost picture of ourselves.

Metaphor, thus, both creates and forecloses. In Laplanche and Pontalis's extrapolation on Lacan, "Forclosure consists in not symbolizing what should have been symbolized" (Laplanche & Pontalis, 1973, p. 166). Whenever an attempted metaphor is not received, and is, thus, silenced, not allowed into language, it is similar to intimating to the interlocutor that he should relinquish that part of his mental life that is concerned with whatever his metaphoric expressions are insistently trying to indicate. This damaging attitude, or incapacity, could induce a patient to retreat perpetually from development by allowing the extinction of more and more vital concerns. Even though constrained by external conditions and biological inheritance, self-formation is also influenced by the demands of the story that the individual is trying to produce. The script itself relies upon metaphoric assumptions that function almost like genes in the process of self-formation. Basic metaphors can be identified which guide one's life journey, shaping a diachronic, enduring structure of the self.

As we constantly use metaphors to expand our relational world, the dynamics of expansion and contraction constitute the polar opposites between which interpretation may oscillate. "The drive towards the formation of metaphors is the fundamental human drive, which one cannot for a single instant dispense with in thought", says Nietzsche, "for one would thereby dispense with man himself" (Nietzsche, 1979, p. 137). Whatever this ultimate drive is, metaphoricity and thinking do not develop automatically and irrespectively of the interactive (psychoanalytic) context within which they originate. For the sake of illustration, let us invoke the case of a young child who is suffering from earache, but has not yet learnt the word for it; he wakes in the middle of the night and walks into his parents' room holding his head and saying, "Mummy, an elephant stepped on my ear." Let us suppose the factual reply is an indifferent, "There are no elephants in this flat." From a maturational perspective, we could think that if the child's metaphor is not interpreted, he might revert to muteness and feel as desperate as a prisoner whose supervisors are forever against him. The situation would be even worse if the small child could have not thought of the metaphor and did not even *dare* to express himself, as if he could not venture to voice a difficulty for fear of retaliation. In this case, from the outside, one could say that nothing had happened and that all was quiet on the front of the child's inner life. But, while earaches may come and go, inner devastations can have lasting effects: in fact, they are the worst form of (pre-Oedipal) mental mutilation.

The richness of nature and culture constantly may be defying conventional classifications. Should such richness tacitly be denied by indirectly endorsing the ultimate value of a literal vocabulary, the individual constrained by it would tend to be excluded from life itself, in as much as a caricature of reality would be enforced upon him. (As in the case of Nirmala—some kind of pet unsuited to *human* life.) Through interpretation, we may create a truly maturational language and, thus, opt for integrative outlooks that we could not formerly envisage. Also, we could develop distrust for former reductive convictions, our obnoxious, definitive stories (as in the case of Nirmala). In analysis, we inexorably move in the direction of discovering that we participate in shaping our life vicissitudes; therefore, we incline more to interaction than to the scrutiny of truth. Consequently, we face an expulsion from the earthly paradise of objective reality, of facts. Even though reality may be very tough and cause us pain, it might, none the less, be a reality for which we are only minimally responsible, for we have only a small effect on something that we simply find out there. This can be very hard for both participants in the analysis. It is often a question of revising perceptions of "very bad" parents or "very mad" patients. In fact, both analysands and analysts use all kinds of metaphors to communicate within the therapeutic setting. This is clearly evidenced by most clinical presentations of interpretative work. From this outlook, we could point to a synoptic view of Freud's use of metaphors; perhaps a linguist would have to work extensively to classify his numerous metaphoric expressions derived from social and political life, from the fields of physical dynamics and hydraulics, anthropology and mythology (Leary, 1990, p. 18). In his use of such metaphors as energy and force, flow and resistance, defence and attack, he probably follows his own research policy of changing metaphors as often as necessary.

The problem of literality

In human interactions—and psychoanalysis is one of them—reciprocity often depends on the hypothesis that most aspects of one's inner life ultimately can be shared. Whenever we injudiciously presume that an interlocutor has no resources for expressing his inner world, we tend to make use of our own metaphoric capacities to give voice to the other's inner experiences. As soon as such a momentous assumption is made within a bi-personal relationship, one of the participants is gradually deprived of the opportunity to exercise his own metaphoric resources. Such an appropriation, moreover, is uniquely unnoticeable *and* difficult to oppose, in as much as it comes across as an interpretative "gift" (Corradi Fiumara, 1995, p. 135). This sort of gift atrophies the symbolic potential of the recipient, who is overcome by the colonising attitude of the more powerful of the two, however responsible that one may be, and opportunities are, thus, gradually usurped. We must, then, increase our understanding of the necessity of metaphor in accessing our otherwise unapproachable inner life. An essentialist, ontological use of our psychological concepts might lead to an inclination to stultify therapy. A critical perception and use of our psychoanalytic vocabulary not only may spare us from some insider jargon, it also spares us from professional forms of insanity, of which there are many. To be bewitched by literality, to fall in love with our sloganised constructs, is probably a form of insanity; it is also the chief hindrance to beneficial interpretation. If we are unable to use the blessing of our metaphoric potential, we can remain stiffened and imprisoned by our literal vocabulary; literality has a very limited function within the psychoanalytic dialogue. For example, if a patient says, "It is cold in this room", and the analyst replies, "There is a blanket on the chair", there would be no analysis at all.

Indeed, there can exist a pathology of literalness (Corradi Fiumara, 1995, p. 55). As the style of ratiocination operating through univocal literal language is orientated towards external reality, events involving inner vicissitudes of psychic suffering may come to appear perplexingly *un*real, with a deadening effect on the analysand. A literal reply to a cry for help is enough to freeze any therapy and instil mute rage, perhaps perpetuating the original trauma of the patient's infancy. The provenance of a literalist inclination could be recognised as a life-damaging compulsion to be acceptably normal; we can perceive this inclination whenever there is a tendency to paraphrase or translate our metaphoric attempts into objective utterances, even at the cost of obliterating original meanings. Should this tendency become dominant to the point of discarding our emerging thoughts, we could become imprisoned within the boundaries of literalness, and deprived of mutative interpretations. When forced to confront complex inner conditions, the atrophy of our metaphoric potential would inevitably pull us into default. As is known, we superficially regard as mentally ill those who do not have a good enough perception of external reality and of interpersonal transactions, but, of course, there should also be a concern for those who are so firmly in contact with standard reality that they ultimately forsake contact with their deeper subjectivity and self-healing efforts. If this attitude predominates and is used to create the illusion of getting rid of unbearable, archaic currents, we will inevitably remain ensnared in a literalist, repetitive pathology. As we know, there are subjects who could even develop a vicarious personality intent only upon being objective and primarily engaged with standard, representational concerns, to the detriment of any awareness of cries for help originating from within. In this sense, then, interpretation is the quintessence of a challenge. Ferro's work on *either* avoiding *or* living emotions offers innumerable examples of different interpretative challenges. Until a patient acquires the ability to manage emotions and the distress that a bond implies, the choice to avoid emotions must be respected (Ferro, 2011, p. 105). And when the bond begins to "grow shoots", Ferro believes that we must refrain from rushing into their clarification and bring them into the transference. In Ferro's words, "One needs rather to be a prudent and trusting gardener who tends their development" (Ferro, 2011, p. 105). With this metaphor, Ferro probably indicates the analyst's capacity to enhance the other's development rather than replace the patient's language with his own language. Imposing the "gift" of one's superior logic amounts to a colonising attitude that asphyxiates the growth of the analysand. At the extreme, we could replace the patient in the management of his own distress—a most infantilising therapeutic policy.

Developing individuals confined within the invisible boundaries of the literal linguistics of adults may persistently seek construals, interpretations, of their metaphoric attempts to communicate; they might often seek this help in very distant interactions or, conversely, might strive to develop the art of a secret intrapsychic dialogue as an alternative to impossible interpersonal exchanges. This is, perhaps, the secret provenance of a vocation to become psychotherapists. An awareness of isolation might dominate one's inner world whenever absence of appropriate interpretation is persistent enough. In whichever context literalness is at a premium, there are positive reinforcements for adaptation to a standard vocabulary; the lack of interest in the interpretation of our metaphoric attempts can be so consistent that whatever cannot be properly said cannot be heard, and ultimately becomes non-existent, unheard of. Thus, pathologic intimacy is *not* attained through creative metaphors but perhaps through destructive relations that might never erupt into overt violence. In fact, these destructive relations are not implemented in attacks on psychic life, but in preventing its expression.

Talking of our human suffering, just think of the difference between the fear of physical mutilation and the terror of psychic deadening. Indeed, the metaphoric capacity is stifled not by inflicting damage to something that exists, but, rather, by obtusely refusing to construe/interpret non-literal messages, ultimately impeding the growth of the mind. The point at issue is not the damage to something that is functioning, but the refusal to allow something to begin to exist and function. "Pain" is a small word for this type of paralysing offence. From this outlook, then, Oedipal vicissitudes linked to the desire to attain something and the concomitant anxiety of retaliation can be viewed as an account in fable form: a visible, "tangible" story of the more crucial (and more difficult to grasp) experiences influencing the development/inhibition of psychic life. *Mutatis mutandis*, these dynamics can even take place in pseudo-therapeutic treatments.

The maturing individual might resort to defensive manoeuvres in order not to sink into a depersonalised condition in which he may only function as a false self whose inchoate expressions have been surrendered to the established managers of language. The nascent personality might resort to any hostile behaviour as a defence against such destructive language games. The individual might intuitively survive by being "bad", since being "good" could be felt as a serious danger to an incipient core of identity. It is possible that anyone suffering from an addiction to literal language may have colluded in being deprived of his own expressive resources (as in the case of Percival). Having relinquished contact with one's own inner roots, one no longer faces the challenge of having to translate messages from the inner world into shareable relations; consequently, the subject restricts his language to elements borrowed from, or imposed by, the authority of the more competent (non-listening) speakers. If this hypothesis is pursued one step further, we may think that those who have been deprived of the opportunity of articulating inner life will identify with educators and ultimately internalise an intrusive and predatory style only suited to depriving still others of the challenge of expressing their inner world (Corradi Fiumara, 1992, pp. 80–108). Whenever the exploration of our inner life is consistently taken over by others, the sort of intimate language for coping with the vicissitudes of hope and despair, attachments and separations may not develop properly. This language may be surrendered to, or usurped by, the superior managers of linguistic expression—however incapable they might be of authentic listening. Such a surrender of profound experiences to the management of individuals perceived to be superior could be seen as colluding with the usurpation of one's inner life. Indeed, the territorial and predatory heritage of our humanisation is thus transferred from the biological to the dialogical level and enacted in the symbolic domain. How is that for inflicting pain?

The voicing of a profound question can in fact be a seminal source of meaning. In his *Tavistock Seminars*, Bion quotes Blanchot, suggesting that *"La réponse est le malheur de la question"* ('The answer is the disease, the misfortune, of the question").

> In other words, the answer is the thing that will put a stop to curiosity better than anything. If anybody is at all curious, you can stuff an answer down his throat or into his ears and that will stop them doing any further thinking. (Bion, 2005, p. 8)

It is nothing less than that. Our thinking for the purposes of affective growth and creativity essentially develops through metaphoric attempts; when these are ignored, it is a stifling insult to the individual. Yet, our innate metaphoricity may still succour us in the face of this danger: our metaphoric potential allows us to remain curious, to craft new questions, and enhance our growth. It is, perhaps, appropriate to invoke Bion further on his view of the relation with the analysand. In his opinion, interpretations can be judged by considering how necessary is the existence of the analyst to the thoughts that he expresses: "The more his interpretations can be judged as showing how necessary *his* knowledge is, *his* character is to the thoughts formulated, the more reason there is to suppose that the interpretation is psychoanalytically worthless" (Bion, 1970, p. 105). Simply worthless, or painfully damaging? Such interpretations, in fact, may be focusing on his own way of seeing things and not on the speciality of the experiences the patient is trying to convey on the basis of a negotiated agreement. For the sake of illustration, think again of the small child with earache, saying that an elephant has stepped on his ear. If the reply by the insufficiently good parent is a factual denial of elephants, the child might eventually recover from an excruciating earache but will hardly recover from the impediment to his expressive life—indeed a form of psychic foreclusion.

The question of psychic effort

The idea of interpretation may generally suggest a smooth, articulate, interactive exchange that, of course, requires accuracy and care. I would like to submit, instead, that interpretation can be very hard work, requiring strenuous effort which simply cannot be avoided. A timely confirmation of this clinical outlook can be found in one of Bion's remarks:

> Although I have plenty of reason to be aware of the defects of the analytic approach, I can't think of anything better. The defects of

psychoanalysis are bound to be *painfully* obvious both to the analyst and the analysand if you are at all sensitive to what is going on, *but I don't know of any way of avoiding that.* There is even the danger in the educational system of supposing that there is a way in which pain can be avoided. (Bion, 2005, p. 54, my emphasis)

This is quite right. However, perhaps we could think of pain in terms of strenuous effort. This part of my work is not organised as a logical sequence of paragraphs leading to a judicious conclusion, but rather as a collection of attempts to show different degrees of intensity in the challenge of interpretation; it is not an exercise for masochists but probably for imaginative, daring athletes. We shall, thus, try to touch upon those aspects of interpretative work that could be described in terms of strenuous psychic effort. At least in part, interpretation is comparable to a sporting encounter. It takes good training, total commitment, and respect for rules. This also means that it is not a translation, a deductive procedure, or a sequential process; it is, in fact, a challenge. Challenges, of course, induce a modicum of inner pain pertaining to the risk of defeat or to a sense of inadequacy. If we do not take good care of the setting, there might be transfers of content, but not the sort of engaging transference that we need for psychoanalytic interpretation. So, we try to bring to light, to auscultate, the demanding quality of interpretative work. At the extreme, if we could for a moment reverse our outlook, and suggest that the humility required for interpretation involves no terrible struggle, but, rather, a creative abandon of our self-adherence which delights in being overwhelmed, we could perhaps see a vague analogy with the mutual surrender of those whom we perceive as lovers (Lewis, 2012, p. 76). This reversal of perspective seems to suggest that psychic effort is not detached from humility—an old-fashioned term, certainly, but perhaps quite appropriate.

Perhaps the theories we use do not matter as much as the practice itself. What we are doing is creating pathways in our consciousness through which healing forces can operate. Necessity, not science, is the beginning of psychoanalytic interpretation. In this connection, think for a moment of physicians, midwives, and sea captains of antiquity. Some of them enjoyed a well-earned reputation while others were considered irresponsible figures. It should be remembered that sea captains used to navigate by the stars, even though their Ptolemaic view of the universe (in which our earth is at the centre of it and the sun revolves around the earth) was certainly wrong. The same is true about theories of physiology and pathology, and yet, some midwives and physicians were rightfully considered responsible and caring. Probably the crux of the problem or the revealing feature of the practice lies in the *way* in which we interpret, in spite of the current, "wrong" theories we have.

However devastating it is, psychic pain is difficult to articulate. Hence, one of the most real aspects of human life is the least suited to be expressed and soar to language: there are hardly words for it. Expression can only be facilitated by the quality of interactive listening. A conjunction of inner pain and isolation is perhaps one of the most severe conditions for the sufferer. The effort involved in interpretation stems from a disposition to touch, and be touched by, primitive, intractable psychic elements. In the language of Ferro, protoemotions are comparable to "dark, lumpy indestructible elements" (Ferro, 2011, p. 125). Also, they occupy and paralyse the psyche "like conglomerates of beta elements waiting for the narrating-dream function to turn them into stories that can be shared" (Ferro, 2011, p. 125). Shared? By whom, and to what extent? It all depends on the analyst's effort to engage in authentic, creative listening. Cancrini asks herself which sensations and which emotions may form in the infantile mind when there is contact with a sadness so deep and deadening that it inevitably pulls the subject into depression and psychosis in spite of parental figures who are sufficiently caring (Cancrini, 2002, p. 48). The problem that she confronts is the missing psychic tissue, the absence of structure. According to Ferro, "It is the working together on the emotions present in the field, *weaving and reweaving them*, which fosters the development of the container/contained through reverie, through unison" (Ferro, 2011, p. 12, my emphasis). (I would also say that this involves the generation of creative metaphors.) Ferro insists that

> All the transformative transitions made session after session lead to an enlargement of the house and the ability to *knit and weave* the protoemotions into pictures, stories, namely the development of a range of skills, not least the ability to contain and to dream. Transference is what continually brings with the protoemotions, the protocontents that will be the raw materials for such transformations. (Ferro, 2011, p. 12)

Cancrini insightfully remarks that together with emotions transformed by the alpha function, and, thus, somehow represented in the mind, there are archaic emotional experiences which have not had such transformation and, as a consequence, have found no expression in dreams or unconscious thoughts; thus, they circulate as unexploded bombs (Cancrini, 2002, p. 35). (Like Sara's perception of her psychotic mother and incestuous brothers; see Chapter Two.) The psychic pain for a possible confrontation with such explosive elements often feels unbearable. In fact, it is not a question of reconstructing insufficiently developed psychic tissue, but of approaching a gaping absence, an undeveloped structure, or something that is too severely deteriorated. Of course, Ferro is thinking of a therapy that does not work on the past and on content, but, rather, focuses on the present and on upgrading the patient's apparatus for thinking—he cares little about *what* (Ferro, 2011, p. 9).

> Protoemotional or emotional forces are often like tsunamis; they cause destruction but they are not aggressive. Their effects come from the uncontainability of the forces involved and sometimes because of inadequate embankments or insufficient storm drains. (Ferro, 2011, p. 8)

In Ferro's view, "What is in excess is the pressure coming from protoemotional states that plead to be collected, contained and transformed" (Ferro, 2011, p. 6). Why? Because they are *too* painful for the patient to bear in their natural state. Of course, in such cases, the mind of the analyst may tend to oppose this kind of intrusion since it involves dealing with extremely dense protoemotional currents. It takes an effort not to boycott this process; it takes old-fashioned hard work.

In her exploration of "Constructions in analysis", Cancrini remarks that, in Freud's view, the psychoanalyst is in a more favourable position than that of the archaeologist because the patient can help in the work of reconstruction. Yet, she argues that the situation is more complex than presented by Freud. In analysis, in fact, we do not simply have to deal with dynamics originating from remote experiences which reappear in transference; in the bi-personal experience of transference, it is not a question of retrieving the memory of lost experiences, but, rather, it is a question of letting ourselves be oppressed, nearly crushed, by experiences which have been lived in a chaotic *and* disintegrating way (Cancrini, 2002, p. 34). It almost feels like an astronomical black hole forever absorbing energy. It feels like a pain that devours psychic life. So, our first challenge is to render somehow visible and expressible that which was not seen or expressed. In our bi-personal field, we must even resort to non-verbal, preverbal contacts. Along with Stern, we could say that without the non-verbal or the preverbal, it would be hard to achieve the empathic, participatory, and resonating aspects of intersubjectivity; in default, one would only be left with a kind of formal, neutral understanding of the other's subjective experience (Stern, 2004, p. 384). Ineffable? Necessary. In this connection, Ferro remarks that he does not wish to give the impression that pre-psychological proto-emotions can be simply transformed into alpha elements or creativity. In fact, he even admits that there are a number of evacuative or para-evacuative activities of our mind that are vital; in his view, there are evacuative discharges of various kinds (Ferro, 2011, pp. 17–18). This can sometimes be observed in the consulting room or in certain so-called evacuative dreams. All of this must somehow be endured and cannot simply be ignored or interpreted away. Even in our everyday life, someone may appear to be seeing what I see, but at the first words a gulf opens between us and we realise that what we see means something totally different to the other; he might be pursuing another vision and cares nothing for our brilliant suggestions. Thus, a strenuous confrontation may occur again. At the extreme, we could be coexisting with a paradox: we could say that an interpretation which is clear and comprehensible might not enlighten the patient at all, while an interpretation that seems somehow incomprehensible, almost ineffable, does somehow enhance the life of the mind.

Cancrini reminds us that there is no "dead mother" in reality, but only a "psychically dead" mother (Cancrini, 2002, p. 36). In Sara's story, this condition can be reconnected to her psychotic mother, who "could become very easily confused". Her mother's illness has never reached the level of a distinct remembrance and remained as an obscured area, unexpressed and inexpressible—blinding. This condition needs to find containment in the mind of the analyst to allow for the expression of what, in the mind of the patient, is still dark, cold, and heavy, something that, at best, can only be communicated by means of projective identification. The patient is looking for someone who can share the derivatives of her unbearable experiences. She requires someone willing to make the effort. Ferro compares these interactions to "dynamite attacks" which should be accepted for their value as a way of communicating despair that otherwise might remain unseen. He adds, "It is, however, probable that excessive quotas of beta elements are in turn driven back, which generates Negative Therapeutic Reaction phenomena or examples of psychotic transference" (Ferro, 2011, p. 81). However, you will ask: can we/you do that for eight hours per day? Also, while a patient has a single analyst to project into with all his might, the analyst has about ten patients who use him/her in a comparable way. While we often think of a bi-personal field in terms of a modicum of reciprocity, the question of the one-to-ten proportion in the affective investment of analysts is hardly ever addressed in literature. Add to this the fact that analysts are intent upon work, while patients are there to save their lives: a challenge indeed.

Although emanating from different perspectives and cultural backgrounds, a convergence can be perceived between the clinical approaches of Ferro and Davies. They both state that aggressiveness is emphatically not something that is bad and the explosiveness of psychic primitive elements is *not* to be confused with aggressive behaviour. In Davies' view, aggressiveness can also work in the service of psychic growth and fight together with our creativity when it is unduly impeded. In so far as it supports creativity, "We can say that aggression is a genuinely constructive force" (Davies, 2012, p. 95). Also, "When the aggressive energies are not allowed to fulfil their proper aim of removing immobilising impediments, they either destructively turn inside or outward against society" (Davies, 2012, p. 96). Ferro insists that "The violence, the explosiveness, the uncontainability of emotions should never be confused with aggression" (Ferro, 2011, p. 6). Aggressive forces are a normal endowment of the species which, in his view, can never be in excess. "What is in excess is the pressure coming from protoemotional states that plead . . . to be transformed" (Ferro, 2011, p. 6). In fact, "Emotional urgency lies behind much behaviour that may on the surface appear aggressive" (Ferro, 2011, p. 8). Increasing clarity on this point can ultimately render the challenge of interpretation more tolerable and more creative.

The experience of relief

Once some terrifying *corpus alienum* is found, touched, and accepted, we may experience some initial sense of psychic relief. We can feel a measure of freedom from the extenuating, futile games of denial or manic compensation, projection or retaliation. Also, we can abandon the belief that we are gradually dying, lost in oblivion and beyond reach. Any genuine psychic touch might even tell us that we might only be running a debilitating fever or suffering from a temporary heart condition. One inchoate form of relief is an incipient psychic confidence that someone seems to understand us: the analysand could, thus, stop feeling like some isolated, incomprehensible monstrosity. We shall, then, try to explore the beneficial influence of some initial, temporary experiences of relief.

Cyrulnik's extensive experience with cases of extreme mental suffering allows him to say that "When despite the suffering a desire is whispered, if only one person hears it, the ember can burst into flame again" (Cyrulnick, 2003, p. 170). It might feel like the permission to breathe. The analyst captures the analysand's distorted attitude to himself, and by this means illuminates the distortions in the patient's relationships with others. It might feel like a knot which is beginning to loosen; it feels like escaping psychic strangulation and gives an inaugural sense of relief. In addition, of course, initial feelings of relief help us to persist on the journey.

We know that development in infancy occurs within the relational context of non-verbal, implicit infant–carer attachment dynamics. But clinicians must do more than observe a hypothetic mother–infant relational pattern. They strive to act as participant observers who join, feel, attune to, and resonate with, the non-verbal, implicit world of affective communications. In the first stages of the analytic journey, it is indeed a relief to begin to sense that an escape is possible from a condition of both captivity and loneliness. This approach dissipates the terror of being too mad to be understood by anyone. It is a preliminary feeling of relief, a sense of respiratory wellbeing. In the view of William James, a suspension of hopeless pain can mark the beginning of something new and not a mere inversion of currents: "Because the sufferer . . . can be saved by what seems to him a second birth, a more lively kind of consciousness than he could enjoy before" (James, 1985, quoted in Davies, 2012, p. 161).

It is interesting to note that both Ferro and Winnicott talk about bullets and guns. According to Ferro, it would be too easy to think of bullets in terms of aggressiveness; for him, "They are explosive protomental states on the point of being evacuated, awaiting only the mental readiness of the other to find a place where they can be contained and transformed" (Ferro, 2011, p. 4). After some analysis, a patient tells Ferro that he feels much better after his father had taken him rifle shooting in the woods. That is, the mental apparatus of the analyst "allows for the modulated explosion of emotions in a way that is somehow contained in a reliable combustion chamber" (Ferro, 2011, p. 4). This is, of course, the beginning of the sort of relief that keeps the patient going. Especially in the early stages of analysis, some initial relief may enhance our effort to move forward. Following Ferro's clinical example, it is clear that it takes a container to attempt any psychological alchemy; it takes a crucible, a vessel, a vase, or a beaker. On the psychic level, that means a very well guarded setting, or even a stable friendship, a habit of concentration, or a room for rehearsal. But a container there must be—indeed, a "combustion chamber", in Ferro's example. In Grotstein's view, "|The rules of the analytic frame are required to vouchsafe the capacity of the two analytic partners to participate with suspension of disbelief in the drama of the passion being uncovered" (Grotstein, 2009, p. 9). If passion and drama are excessively painful and not sufficiently contained by analytic *rules*, one may, of course, resort to some condition of inner paralysis, as if saying, "It feels even worse if I try to move." Analysis can be a school of creative suffering, and a successful one, because it constantly adapts to the demands of the current resources of the analysands. Grotstein again:

> Their inability to tolerate frustration may . . . be due to insufficient tolerance of their affect display as infants by mothers who could not be able *containers*, which is also a way of saying that they were subject to *disorganizing attachment* to their objects. (Grotstein, 2009, p. 66)

When the alternative is offered, one can immediately feel some initial sense of relief.

As we know, there are different interpretations that can be given as a response to the same communication and we could not possibly say that only one of them is correct. Different analysts generate different interpretations and the same analyst may give different interpretations at different times. The differences primarily depend upon the degree of anxiety that is at work in the dyad: anxiety as a signal of the arrival of beta elements that we have not yet metabolised, or it can be the prelude to elaboration (Ferro, 2011, p. 81). And thus, paradoxically, the disquieting prospect of transformation gradually lightens the burden of anxiety. In Ferro's view, "If the signals of anxiety are not immediately picked up and metabolised, this can activate the projection of the beta screen, a last resort to generate countertransference and to see one's protoemotional states accepted" (Ferro, 2011, p. 81). Strong manoeuvres, indeed. Also, "It is not a question of reinforcing or criminalising the defence mechanism, but of making it gradually less and less necessary by progressively negotiating the 'lava lump'" (Ferro, 2011, p. 98). Thus, the patient is no longer alone with it, no longer lonely under its crushing weight. Ferro continues,

> Of course this can take quite a long time; the defensive constellations of the analyst are also called into play, and the work of emotional re-weaving can be carried out either in a grey, technical way or with dynamism and creativity. This reflects the qualities of the analytic couple; but equally I would say . . . it reflects the qualities of the analytic group one belongs to. (2011, p. 99)

When a symbolic milieu is created for knowing that we are in distress, this knowing allows for a still place that surrounds the conflict in an accepting way: indeed, a talking cure that replaces the combative or nihilistic outlook, an initial relief from a state of cold, freezing war. This may begin to tentatively transmute our thick, strangling entanglements. What interpretations can initially do is to create a space for transformation to happen. This incipient realisation interrupts the asphyxiating trend. With this outlook of creative integration, Rosenfeld recommends that at certain very intense, or painful, moments, we should clearly remind the patient that he is the knowing, the knower, not the devastating condition that is being known. At the appropriate time, we should directly tell the analysand something like this: "You are not the same as what you are talking about; the *real* you is *now* talking to me clearly and confidently, and that is who you truly are; you are not the madness that you share with me, you are the one who dares to do the showing and the sharing" (Rosenfeld, Rome Seminars, 1975–1985). It is a liberation to realise that the persecutory voice in my head is not who I really am. Who am I then? The one who tries to know and share all that. This is the supporting awareness that is prior to analytic thinking, the psychic space in which thoughts and dire emotions may come to expression. If evil has any reality (and it has relative, not absolute, reality), this is its enactment: complete identification with persecutory thought forms, with unbearable emotional forms. This results in a total unawareness of one's connectedness with every other, with any other. When this connectedness is really felt, the relief from pain becomes almost tangible. You are the one who speaks to me, you are not the "lava lump", the unthinkable, primitive, concrete thing. Rosenfeld again: the one who articulates the uneasiness of being caught in repetitive difficulties is not quite *entirely* caught; he can share his imprisoning tangles with a witnessing, accepting other and by doing so the patient does not collude with the sickly tangle (Rosenfeld, Rome Seminars 1975–1985).

Words, irrespective of whether they are vocalised or remain unspoken thoughts, may cast an almost hypnotic spell upon our distressed inner world. One can easily lose oneself in them, become hypnotised into believing that when one has attached a word to something one knows what it is. The fact is that we do not know what it is. We have only covered the misery with a label. It is a preliminary relief to work with someone who does see that, who does not share that sort of policy, and who tries to remove or rename the mental labels. This perception creates an atmosphere of relief that may enhance the healing process. In the course of years, Rosenfeld highlights the intense pleasure/joy of beginning to function well mentally, to function creatively, in direct contrast to the bitter sadness of repetitive thinking, rigidity, and untruth. In the present work, we are constantly dealing with the discovery of *psychic* truth and of ways to live with it, and this resonates with one of Pascal's remarks: "Others are too near, too far, too high or too low. In painting, the rules of perspective decide it, but how will it be decided when it comes to truth and morality?" (Pascal, 1995, p. 1). This, indeed, is the question, if truth points to psychic health and "morality" points to our coexistential condition.

CHAPTER EIGHT

Moving forward

The idea of forward moving

Psychoanalysis is primarily about *somehow* moving forward psychically through pain, or in spite of it. Thus, a variety of subtitles come to mind as possible pointers to this topic. These could be *Rafta, rafta* or *Yalla, yalla*; "More or less slowly", or "Less or more quickly". Whichever caption we might choose will do, because the general idea is that we try to move forward, at our own pace, or even perhaps taking pauses in our ongoing effort to move on psychically. It is an effort to (re)gain some freedom to progress into the future. In fact, we do not know why we would choose to turn our back on the future and remain petrified in the past. Initially, though, it takes a refusal to heed oracular voices of any kind, whether grandiose or punishing, inner or outer. Contrary to what might be believed, one thing is very unlikely in psychic life: the capacity to remain stationary (Thiele Rolando, 1982, p.101). The incapacity to suffer life creatively can ultimately be a defence against the analytic process, or against any process. But then, if the analysand or the analyst cannot endure transformations, there will be futile, lamentable attempts to immobilise the situation. And we do not achieve any authentic psychic life whenever our complaints ultimately promote inertia, when what we really need is to build up momentum. Perhaps, possibility is far more frightening than impossibility, and freedom is far more terrifying than any imprisonment. As we know, towards the end of analysis patients may even confront a fear of being well, that is, the freedom to live.

Any form of therapy is a risk and no guarantees are given. We finally accept that time is limited and that we cannot waste it ruminating about the past or fantasising about the future. The only thing that matters is what we are doing at the moment. The *here and now* principle of psychoanalytic interpretation seems to endorse just this outlook. To move forward, we might have to become one with our journey. The younger we are, the more frustrated we can be by any absence of clarity and the presence of paradox. The older we are, the more likely it will be that we can tolerate paradox and the strain that it generates. Thus, we might come to realise that our life journey is our actual home, and that the quality of the home is a function of the paradoxes that we can tolerate. We might have to face the conclusion that the journey itself is our only possible home.

The idea of therapy as a painstaking itinerary towards maturity is essentially based on an understanding of moving forward through creative suffering. This has already been adumbrated by Freud in *Beyond the Pleasure Principle*, where he says that "If we cannot move on 'flying' we can slowly proceed limping" (Freud, 1920g, p. 64). Maturity is a metaphor originating from the blooming and ripening that we observe in nature. "Maturation" might sound like an antiquated term, but it is perhaps the right one; it also connotes the support that comes from something greater than we are, and indicates that one's forward motion towards maturity puts one in synchrony with the greater movement of nature and culture, enabling us to avail ourselves of the myriad opportunities it can provide. This unforeseen guidance is one of the many benefits that a maturational journey can grant us. You cannot control maturation intellectually from the outside; somehow, you have to *enter* maturational processes in order to tap into their energy. The modern mind typically misunderstands any maturational journey: it wants to make it predictably controllable. What we should rather do is join in it. If we are to be cured by analysis, we are also to experience the psychic forces sustaining our life, shaping us for growth.

Of course, we cannot prove the existence of "maturational forces", but, as we move forward, we no longer feel the need to do so. What we want is to progress. A sense of purpose does not come from thinking about maturation; it comes from psychic actions that move you towards the future. The moment you do this, you activate a force more powerful than the desire to avoid pain. Psychoanalysis is a practice rather than the study of books. It takes courage; it requires the endurance of psychic pain in the attempt to break free of defensive subjugations. In this connection, we could invoke the story of a "method" for catching monkeys. It is reported that certain monkeys are so ingenious that they have worked out that if they insert an arm into the narrow neck of an amphora, they will be able to get the food that they can smell at the bottom of it. This is very clever of them. However, they will not abandon this strategy even when they realise that they are unable to pull out their arm with a *closed* hand full of food. They can then be caught by their even smarter companions—the humans who set up the amphora with the food. But then, are we really smarter when it concerns our own affairs? Perhaps we, the wizards, cannot give up performing our best tricks, our most successful games—even our *jeux de massacre*. Imagine a monkey with insight saying, "I don't care if I cannot regain my freedom; I don't want to lose what I have won because it is just too painful".

In the light of the journey metaphor, we could perhaps say that the Israelites traversing the desert were worn out by hunger and thirst when they declared their nostalgia for the meat and onions that they could occasionally enjoy in their servitude in Egypt. Whether or not we can attain happiness (some kind of promised land), it is clear that no inner emancipation can be achieved without some endurance of psychological deserts. It is significant to recall that when servitude was abolished in post-Tzarist Russia, not all of the people who were bought or inherited together with the land were ready to opt for an independent, free life—especially if they had good masters. Enduring servitude in unproductive pain might only serve to degrade oneself into a thing-like, inanimate creature, only able to fight back in a self-defeating way. Yet, any opposition to injustice seems to require clear articulation and reasoned scrutiny in both states, servitude and freedom. It takes endurance to tolerate both of them for emancipatory purposes.

We might like to think of ourselves as finished products, complete on our own, but we are not. To be whole, we need to stay connected to some maturational journey because, perhaps, we can never be more than a work in progress. Therapy repairs our connection to maturational forces, and perhaps this is the reason why it works. But the connections are not permanent; they break again and again. Hollis (2003) asks, if we are to use the metaphor of life as a journey at all, then whither are we going? We could ask what the goal is, the *raison d'être* for this strenuous effort. Our best answer is that, paradoxically, the purpose *is* the journey itself, not the destination. As we come to realise that the journey is our home, we also come to appreciate that the psychic quality of this home is a function of the inner paradoxes that we can tolerate. Through his unquestionable acumen, Winnicott provides an enlightening presentation of the function of paradox:

> I am drawing attention to the *paradox* involved in the use by the infant of what I have called the transitional object. My contribution is to ask for a *paradox* to be accepted and tolerated and respected, and for it not to be resolved. It is possible to resolve the *paradox*, but the price of this is the loss of the value of the *paradox* itself. The *paradox* has value for every individual who is capable of being infinitely enriched by the exploitation of the cultural link with the past and with the future. (Winnicott, 1971, p. xii, my emphasis)

It may be noted that, with total disregard of style, in these few lines Winnicott uses the term "paradox" *five* times, as if he were somehow striving to infuse its value into the reader; it is a quasi-performative statement rather than a merely informative sentence.

Our forward moving is never entirely painless; in Bion's words, "Of all the hateful possibilities, growth and maturation are feared and detested most frequently" (Bion, 1970, p. 53), and he insists that the central point appears to be the painful nature of change in the direction of maturity. Perhaps there is no point in asking why the intensity of pain bears so little relationship to the seriousness of recognisable danger. "There is no doubt that mental pain in particular is feared in a way that would be appropriate if it corresponded directly to the mental danger. The relationship of pain to danger is, however, obscure" (Bion, 1970, p. 53). For instance, what is concluded at any given moment is subsequently superseded by the expansion of the situation to include different values. Perhaps some "depression" we had back then, the conflict that yesterday seemed unbearable, may become the catalysts for growth in the next stage of the journey. We cannot expect answers for how we might outgrow them tomorrow, only to be confronted with new questions. Pain, moreover, has no tendency, in its own right, to proliferate. When it is over, it is simply finished, and the natural sequel is an inclination to joy. Conversely, after a perverse solution and its derivative effect on life, one seems obliged to go back and somehow stop the spreading damage: a laborious undoing seems necessary. Pain requires no such undoing. Psychic pain is, perhaps, free of that proliferous tendency which is the worst characteristic of perversion. The ending of pain leaves us ready to freely move forward.

According to Ferro, psychoanalysis moves from being a psychology of contents, conflicts, or deficiencies to being "a psychoanalysis of experiences/instruments that foster the very development of the possibility/capacity to think" (Ferro, 2011, p. 86). In Ferro's view, an analysis that focuses on content, or that activates it before developing apparatuses for thinking it, could become a psychoanalysis that sets off iatrogenic pathologies, that cannot insert patients into their own forward movement (Ferro, 2011, p. 86). We need support in our moving forward. Phillips' acumen calls our attention to the fact that Winnicott often writes of "hold*ing*, us*ing*, play*ing*, relat*ing*, feel*ing* real", and remarks that "the prominence of verbal nouns reflects Winnicott's preoccupation with process (rather than conclusion)" (Phillips, 1988, p. 14). The beneficial effort of moving forward as a response to difficult emotions involves inner advantages. We do not become aggrieved if something does not turn out to be a success because there is some subjacent awareness that, at the moment of action, we have done all we could do, that we never entirely surrendered our agency. It is perhaps appropriate here to invoke Symington's question: "What is this step that I wish to make but dare not? It is a step into a void, into nothingness, into a place of no guarantees, safety, or security" (Symington, 2004, p. 179). This step can, of course, be retarded because we are not obliged to jump forward; we may just struggle along at a very slow pace—our own pace.

We shall turn now to Davies' multi-faceted contribution to the question of moving forward through pain, or in spite of it. He suggests that we suffer when we fight to change a psychic condition into a form that will serve our growth (Davies, 2012, p. 40). In synthesis, this is the suffering that accompanies us when we wilfully sacrifice one primitive (schizo-paranoid) attitude for a different one in the hope that the new position (perhaps more depressive) will serve us better in our forward moving. To ensure that transformations succeed, we will have to learn to abandon some of our old, cherished habits and develop new ones. In Davies' view, this requires a capacity to endure the confusion and loneliness of not belonging anywhere, of traversing a bleak no-man's-land, of learning a new world while at the same time grieving the old (Davies, 2012, p. 42). We must experience the loss of the known while having no clear route to guide us into the future. The pain of changing habitual conditions into those serving our deeper needs ("best interests"), is the pain of moving step by step from the refuge of the past, however restrictive, towards the promise of the future, however uncertain. Maturation through dealing with pain requires our constant self-trust; we have to believe that following our own personal, deeper inclinations is just as worthy as our tendency to submit to the authorities of our culture, or perhaps it is even better. It is the possibility of straying into areas remote from any chartered course, even if these remote places elicit the suspicion and warnings of the co-citizens of our so called "comfort zones" (Davies, 2012, p. 67). And whatever the problem or the query we pursue, what defines our journey always derives from a source deep within us. The problem usually pertains to our unique life stories, experiences, and struggles; because of this, it often feels more urgent and alive than the problems posed to us by an external authority, even those emanating from the core of our most prestigious theorists and/or clinicians. Davies also insists that formal education (our most highly valued schooling) does not in the least prepare us to use psychic pain, and move on. Lifelong self-education, as theorised by Corradi and Madia (2003), is the only feasible alternative to formal education. In fact, in contrast to formal education, our maturation is the lifelong process through which we confront a problem that is critical to our personal lives, a problem for which we seek answers by way of our own self-created strategies. If education does not result in a lifelong process, it is no education at all.

I believe that perhaps Christopher Columbus, in his perilous journey to the Indies, must have taken into account the possibility of not reaching some final destination, the possibility of no return, or of disappearing into oblivion. These hypotheses become tolerable only if somehow stated and accepted. If such a journey will involve anguish and tribulation, a modicum of preliminary awareness might create the possibility of tolerance and integration; of course, the "journey" is one of the most common images utilised to refer to the course of our lives. But perhaps the Genoese sailor, unlike his astute Greek predecessor from Ithaca, was not a psychological hero of cunning and curiosity. He was more inclined to sailing and exploration. But then, he was a very well trained sailor, so experienced that he was capable of catching propitious eastern winds to go to America, *and* propitious winds to return to Europe. The rationale is that we need the humility to undertake a very serious training and constantly prepare ourselves to cope with adversity: it is not simply a matter of luck, inspiration, or curiosity; preparation is needed. Many others, perhaps, tried before Columbus, but did not painstakingly organise their attempts to coincide with the propitious winds. A tolerance of inner pain and conflict is primarily based on awareness and integration—ultimately, on a very good professional training. This is probably the way to move towards new frontiers and to leave behind the gilded prison of our anaesthetised lives.

We have a natural desire for a relationship with higher maturational forces: it is so strong that it can never be completely eradicated. Current consumerism preys on this desire and misdirects it by convincing us that the propellent of development exists *inside* tangible objects or social positions *outside* of us: from the fruit of a forbidden tree to the sexualised conjunction with a special parent, from a very specific social rank to a very particular pin, title, badge, from ingestible foods to superior theories. The ubiquitous search for super remedies surrounds us all the time, while disillusionment is inevitable. But then, as long as we can use it, even disillusionment could actually turn into a inducement to move forward.

Negotiating (with) painful emotions

A biological organism can get rid of toxic, non-metabolisable substances quite independently of other living beings. When it comes to human psychic life and mental states, however, we absolutely need *others* to absorb and embody toxic elements. Of course, we can evacuate into our bodies (our individual, innocent bodies which can hardly revolt against an oppressive mind) in the form of psychosomatic illness or else, preferably, into the communal, social body in the forms of delinquency and collective stupidity. This is a central problem in our human condition. There are inner currents that are too explosive with respect to any processing apparatus, and so we dislodge them into *others* for the purpose of developing a tranquillity based on hatred directed outside of us. As soon as one resentment fades, another takes its place. We could call it "Resentment in search of a cause", like Pirandello's characters in search of an author (*Sei personaggi in cerca d'autore*). Ultimately, all we can do is help, and be helped, to contain and process unbearable, negative affects. We can often aid the other to transform murderous attitudes into narratives that can be de-concretised and rewoven. In our human species there are innumerable ordinary geniuses who are especially good at supporting the psychic metabolism of others.

Paradoxically, our immemorial history of civilisation is also, to a large extent, a history of human pathology. If the history of humanity were the clinical case history of a single human being, the diagnosis would come close to "chronic paranoid delusions", "pathological propensity to acts of violence against perceived enemies", or else, "clinically insane with a variable rate of lucid intervals of peace". In our times, the demand for relationship is urgent and compulsive, the more so as a sense of community has become eroded in human groups. Yet, the paradox remains, as we will see, that the single best thing we can do to improve our relationships is to work on ourselves, to relieve the other from the impossible agenda of the expectations we bring upon them, to remove from them the burden of our own destiny.

Dealing with archaic, overwhelming emotions can take different forms. There are patients whose pre-analytic psychic lives even utilised different living creatures—animals, for example—to deal with primitive affects. One patient, for instance, was totally involved with cats; another patient was completely committed to wolves; a third one had a long-time passion for reptiles. In the early phases of analysis, they expressed most of what they had to say through cats, wolves, and snakes. Of course, patients, as is well known, have already tried in different, often strenuous, ways to cure themselves before coming to analysis. Their own self-treatment can sometimes be ineffective, while, in other cases, primarily might be in need of further development and integration, as in the case of the three patients that are briefly presented. Perhaps, when they felt misunderstood, it was precisely that they felt overwhelmed by their ambivalences toward the thinkable and unthinkable aspects of inner "cats", "wolves", and "snakes". But what does an elegant word such as "overwhelmed" really mean? Perhaps it can actually mean paralysed, crushed, devoured, killed. This causes immense pain. This pervasive pain must be dealt with, must be faced, through appropriate passions. The patients had all reported difficult stories that included rejecting and intrusive parents: perhaps something too painful to mentalize in any endurable way. They brought their "animals" into analysis to seek a way of creating a dialogue with the proto-emotions that the animals somehow represented. A very large part of what they tried to tell me came via their beloved creatures. As subjects who attempted to negotiate with their most difficult emotions, they sought therapeutic help to pursue their negotiations in a more creative and less punishing way. The driving force of the story is the need to find a space–time in which to be helped to develop the capacity to think and share that which cannot be properly said (Ferro, 2011, p. 11).

One patient, who had finally become an acclaimed authority on wolves, talked about them most of the time, and a second patient who was a successful child psychotherapist talked about cats quite regularly. The third one, who had an enduring passion for reptiles and especially for snakes, also talked about them all the time. Their diversified stories about wolves, cats, and snakes were personal and surprising. They needed to integrate affects expressed through canines, felines, and reptiles into their lives, and into our joint venture. They brought the fuel for the work, but the analyst provided a significant transfer of what was developed in the bi-personal field back to the patients, who became gradually more capable of transforming their difficult aspects into daily creativity. Their emotions had existed vicariously through their animals.

The wolf expert had problems with his own destructiveness that sometimes mainfested in somatisations, or that he projected on the external world through omnipotent, successful ventures. He also had at least two or three girlfriends at the same time but was forever unable to settle with one. He had an actual smell of animals on him all the time. He found wolves in unexpected places in the countryside, and also requisitioned illegally kept wolves. When he found a wolf killed by a firearm, he lobbied for the acceptance of wolves in innumerable villages and made every effort to enforce the legal ruling that farmers whose livestock was killed by wolves must be fully reimbursed by their local authorities. He repopulated areas in which wolves had become extinct. He was an activist against superstitious, persecutory beliefs concerning wolves. He often thought of bringing me some adorable cub to hold and cuddle for a moment.

The child psychotherapist lived with cats, cured sick cats, collected and rehomed cats, imposed cats on others, performed euthanasia on terminally ill cats, and even took care of female cats that killed or rejected their offspring. She often had the phantasy of bringing a cat into a session for me to adopt or even just see; she even had a theoretical, remote interest in related creatures such as leopards and tigers. She mentioned that once she nearly "died" upon encountering a well-to-do and elegant female cousin and she felt almost annihilated; she said she only saved her life because she was wearing a bright yellow coat that made her *feel* like a cat.

The man who liked snakes had become president of some international reptile society. He had always suffered from being aloof, reserved, cold, and shy with women, to the point of actually begging for sexual contact. He earned a good living as a dentist. He could not remember how and when he developed an interest in snakes. His interest grew steadily in the course of his adolescent years and he became an expert, to the point that he was consulted about different health problems in snakes. He was fascinated by all kinds of snakes, from the superb mambas to the impressive anacondas, or the intriguing cobras. He even collected snakes that lived at his home, albeit only small ones and strictly non-poisonous. He had no difficult in finding snakes in different places and also shipped them by regular post, the small ones within nylon stockings stocked with fruit and snacks. On the outside of these parcels he always indicated the exact nature of the content: "Reptiles". Aside from sexual interpretations and concerns, he definitely wanted me to help him cope with his archaic emotional snakes. At one point in his analysis, he offered to bring me a little light-skinned snake. Of course, I insisted that I wanted to interact with his inner affects, of which these wonderful animals were a representation.

De Monticelli remarks that we may gradually become accustomed to preventing our hearts from being even slightly touched by whatever might be hurtful or disquieting; we are all less or more proficient in our capacity to neutralise experience (De Monticelli, 2003, p. 278). Affective acceptance lies at the opposite end of this attitude. By being hospitable to potentially threatening contacts, almost to the point of submitting to them, we actually come to see and perceive them, and then we can no longer eliminate what we see, just as we cannot avoid seeing an object in front of us, once we have recognised it. But, of course, there is no obligation to keep our eyes open; by not seeing, we can behave as if things were not there. In the psychic domain, the price for this blinding attitude is a drastic loss of insight—a detrimental diminution of inner life. By opposing it, we can hope, with Winnicott, "to keep in touch with our primitive selves whence the most intense feelings and even fearfully acute sensations derive" (Winnicott, quoted in Phillips, 2005, p. 92). It is a question of seriously accepting cats and wolves and snakes.

Vulnerability is the acceptance of more and more elements to process. If we do not want to elaborate them, we just do not perceive them and exclusion becomes automatic—as if foreclosure were established as an epistemic rule. Psychoanalytic theories offer different views of psychic development going wrong. One of the points of emphasis is that our basic processing capacities can be damaged; when this happens, our ability to digest, to metabolise, both emotional nutrients *and* poisons is injured. In Eigen's view, the ultimate paradox of our psychic vicissitudes is that we can be damaged by bonds that give us life, disabled by relations that help us grow, succoured by contacts that hurt us (Eigen, 2001, p. 1). However, even if the capacity to include and absorb may make us vulnerable, perhaps we have more to gain from vulnerability than from exclusionary, defensive control of situations.

Painless sanity, as an ultimate superficial quality of life, is a caricature of mental life. In Phillips' language, "For the more deeply sane, whatever else sanity might be, it is a container of madness, not a denier of it" (Phillips, 2004, p. 121). As is known, when too much is excluded, it is not sane to be normal, and we might ultimately turn into McDougall's "normotic" creatures (McDougall, 1990). Creativity can freely expand where there is a shift away from a controlling knowledge and towards a propensity for inclusion—even at the cost of becoming vulnerable, of accepting an excess of psychic currents. In the domain of psychoanalysis, there is little interest in external success: its goal is to develop inner strength. We usually care about what we achieve on the outside; psychoanalysis is interested in who we are inside. The victim subject thinks he knows how the universe should work, but when it does not treat him in the way he deserves, he concludes that the world is against him. This becomes his rationalisation for giving up and retreating into a defence system where he can stop trying. But then, even in everyday life, we do not get what we deserve; we only get what we negotiate.

The "teens" transition

As psychoanalysts, we can hardly draw from, or even approach, the scientific story of our neurological transformations, and must be content with "popular" science. In the simplified renditions of our brain's physiology, we are told that sophisticated scanning systems demonstrate significant brain changes in the course of adolescence. The suggestion I submit is that if we cannot cope psychically with these transformations and/or we suffocate adolescence by means of legal or illegal drugs, with absolutist ideologies, drastic oppression, and the like, we are prevented from gaining the benefits of this ulterior neurological maturation. In other words, if adolescence is unbearable on the psychic level and is somehow suppressed, we may not engage with beneficial organismic changes. We might be thrown into adult life with insufficient neurological equipment—a sad prospect indeed. *The National Geographic* presents an article by David Dobbs which is entitled "Beautiful brains", the general title on the front cover being "The new science of the teenage brain" (Dobbs, 2011, p. 43). We are told in this presentation that, as we move through adolescence, the brain undergoes significant remodelling and a wiring upgrade. Dobbs suggests that, taken together, "These changes make the entire brain a much faster and more sophisticated organ ... At the same time, the frontal areas develop greater speed and richer connections allowing it to generate ... more variables and agendas than before" (Dobbs, 2011, p. 48). When these innovations proceed successfully, we become better at regulating impulse, desire, goals, self-interest, rules, ethics, and even altruism; ultimately, we generate behaviour that is more complex and, sometimes at least, more sensible. Dobbs emphasises, however, that at times, and especially at first, the brain does this work *clumsily*: "It is hard to get all those new cogs to mesh" (Dobbs, 2011, p. 49). Adolescence can be very painful for the teenagers and for carers who do not quite know how to utilise all that transformative distress. It can be enlightening for our purposes to try to think of this period in terms of further neurological development; this cannot be impeded, for its default might result in irreversible damage—nothing less than that. But then, what goes on in the brain and how are we to cope with it on the psychic level? The question is, of course, how we can endure these changes and how we can utilise them. When we attempt to evolve without responding appropriately to inner physiological turmoil, we can miss an important maturational step. We are in need of an adolescence that is lived through its necessary neurological transformations and which is not suppressed or anaesthetised.

Titles from scientific literature and popular articles about the "teen brain" present the view that, with adolescents, it is a question of work in progress in immature brains; so much so that some ask the question of whether they are in a state "akin to mental retardation" (Dobbs, 2011, p. 48), a retardation of which they have a measure of awareness, an inner discomfort that they must cope with and somehow utilise. Dobbs reminds us that selection is hell on dysfunctional traits. If adolescence is essentially a collection of them—angst, idiocy, and haste, impulsiveness, selfishness, and reckless bumbling—then how did those traits survive selection? They could not if they were not the period's most fundamental or consequential features. But the more we learn about what really makes this period unique, the more adolescence starts to seem like a highly functional, even adaptive, period. The resulting account of the adolescent brain—call it the "adaptive adolescent story"—casts the teenager less as a rough draft than as an exquisitely sensitive, highly adaptable creature wired almost perfectly for the task of moving from the safety of comfort zones into the challenging world outside. This is quite a passage in a life journey in which we struggle to move forward.

Brain imaging technology enables us to actually *see* the teenage brain in sufficient detail. These imaging tools provide a new way to ask an old question—what is wrong with these youngsters?—and reveal an answer that surprises almost everyone (Dobbs, 2011, p. 43). Our brains, it turns out, take much longer to develop than we had thought. This revelation suggests both a simplistic, unflattering explanation of teenagers' maddening behaviour, *and* a more complex, affirmative explanation as well. Dobbs concludes that the brain is still developing and that adaptation is painstaking. Once again, we are forcibly drawn into a confrontation with the question of inner pain and psychic suffering. Only those who can endure the tsunamis of adolescence will gain maturationally. But the path for moving forward is a very narrow one. In Dobbs' words, "The game rewards risk-taking. Thus the game rewards you for taking a certain risk but punishes you for taking too much" (Dobbs, 2011, p. 54). The long, slow, back-to-front developmental wave, completed only in our mid-twenties, appears to be a uniquely human adaptation. It might be one of the most consequential. It can seem a bit crazy that we humans do not wise up a bit earlier in life. But if we became smart sooner, we would end up more stupid. Once again, the capacity to tolerate the discomfort is the key to a successful transition.

There are situations that make us vulnerable and we avoid them like the plague. We never want to give anyone the chance to inflict pain on us. However, we pay a high price for it, for we can even sacrifice a maturational career; we might not give it up totally, but there is hardly anyone who has not given up something to avoid pain. We barricade ourselves behind an invisible wall and do not venture out beyond the wall for fear of being hurt. This safe place might be called a "comfort zone". For most of us, the comfort zone is not a physical place; it is a way of life that avoids anything that might be too painful. In the light of the recently discovered neurological transformations of adolescence, we could say that the price we pay for our so-called comfort zones is drastically unaffordable: it even compromises our psycho–physical integration.

In simple words, we could say that people who are non-avoiders actually do better than others. They are less intimidated by the world, more satisfied with their own efforts. Of course, it is easier to associate with people who are not a threat, but this is really a form of avoidance that keeps us from living as fully as we could. An effective leader, for instance, can tolerate the displeasure of others. Of course, we want creativity, maturation, growth, and the only way to connect to them is to engage in forward motion. To do just that you must face psychic earthquakes, and be able to move past them. In a synoptic outlook on these dramatic maturational passages, we could even think of making efforts to align with whatever healthy, creative energies there might be in the community; it seems that we need a strenuous search for such sources of evolutionary courage. If we think of our interpersonal universe as some kind of energy field in which we are immersed and by which we are formed, accepting uncomfortable challenges might transform the person from something randomly fluctuating in that field to a more fully functioning, more conscious part of that psychological eco-system. If we cannot grow in reasonable harmony with our organismic transformations, we might primarily generate intoxicating behaviour—just think of the *rage* that would be generated by getting bigger and bigger without really growing.

We hear, for instance, that some countries are more responsible than others for pollution and environmental degradation. Similarly, in any micro- or macro-community, some individuals are psychically more intoxicating than others. So, we need a profound revision of our concepts of interpersonal equity and balance: only certain levels of intoxication are tolerable and a certain level of pathogenic emissions cannot be exceeded. But then, some individuals are more efficient than others at enduring and processing intoxicating experiences. Psychoanalysis is one of the attempts to co-operate in the metabolism of archaic emotions that paralyse the mind. And there are always ordinary geniuses who secretly do the detoxifying job for others. In Oliver's view, in fact, creativity is equated to an antidote for the degrading damages inflicted on psychic spaces which ultimately impede the movement of drives towards signification—that is, psychic life and humanisation (Oliver, 2004, p. 162).

CHAPTER NINE

Psychic growth

Pain and psychic growth

To try to show that through psychic pain we can enhance inner emancipation, we could invoke here a medieval story. We could also ask, "Emancipation from what?" From archaic, intolerable emotions that can impede the life of the mind and which must be somehow metabolised. However unavoidable, psychic pain is, in fact, so bitter and dreadful that we do not want to go through it, or even try to see any further across it. But perhaps we could. The *Divine Comedy*, a very popular poem written in "vulgar" Italian rather than in "noble" Latin, is meant, in fact, to be instructive for all. Dante says:

> In the middle of the journey of our life I came to myself in a dark wood where the straight way was lost.
> Ah! how hard a thing it is to tell what a wild, and rough, and stubborn wood this was, which in my thought renews the fear!
> So bitter is it, that scarcely more is death: but to treat of the good things that I there found, I will relate the other things that I discerned.
>
> (Alighieri, 1958, *Canto* 1).

In fact, he discerned a great deal by going through it. At the end of the visit to all kinds of torments, indeed an infernal journey, we can perhaps come to perceive "the beauteous things which Heaven bears"; and then we can issue out again "to see the stars". Dante proceeds forward in spite of a bitterness that "scarcely more is death". But why go through all that hell? Because the poet wants to show us the good things that he discovered there. Dante's goal is to actually share with us the creative, beautiful aspects of the journey and, ultimately, arrive to share in the love that moves our "dancing" universe.

In everyday life, we are often asked to confront our suffering, to wrestle with it, though it brings us at first even more pain. In any maturational process, the initial steps can be the more painful ones, and any enjoyment may come only when proficiency and fluency are acquired. But what if an aversion prevails to these rough and tough first steps? We might be tempted to give up any inner action and repeatedly struggle with further repetitive reactions. Paradoxically, even the vicissitudes of love, with its innumerable overwhelming emotions, are known to be connected with vulnerability and pain proportional to the joy that is being sought. If we assume that the emotions that we abhor and try to avoid are the very painful ones, we can endorse Ferro's significant statement: "I would like to offer some reflections on how the *avoidance* of emotions [painful ones, especially] is one of the main activities of our mind" (Ferro, 2011, p. 1). These activities, however, are essentially reactive and certainly not proactive. In Ferro's words,

> It is no longer a question of analysis seeking to lift the veil of repression by means of interpretative work. Here psychoanalysis looks to develop the tools necessary to foster the development and production of thought itself, that is the apparatus for dreaming and thinking. (Ferro, 2011, p. 62)

This is probably in view of generating actions that are not simply reactions to unbearable affects.

From a different, more anthropological, perspective, Davies suggests that the emotion of aggressiveness might become destructive when it is de-routed from the function of eliminating blocks that inhibit us in our life journey; that is, when it is prevented from creatively removing obstacles to our development: "In this instance the aggressive energies, not being allowed to fulfil their proper aim of removing immobilising impediments, may either destructively turn inward against the individual or turn outward against society" (Davies, 2012, p. 96). The most vivid image comes from Hollis, where he says, "Though it pull our bone from its socket, as with Jacob, we must not let go the Angel of Suffering until it blesses us" (Hollis, 2003, p. vii). Growth is no joke; it is a passage, but, of course, some of us might choose not to move forward.

In this journey we call our life, we are best served not by answers, which are but a seductive offer of relaxation and pause, at best, but by the questions that disturb us into growth. In Ferro's view of psychoanalytic work, different symptoms or different attachments indicate different ways of facing the same problem: dealing with intractable emotions. One hopes that "These emotions become encased into acceptable stories, choices and propensities" (Ferro, 2011, p. 102). The unprocessed proto-emotions determine a generalised psychic atmosphere which is asphyxiating, toxic, deadening. Referring to a patient with a psychotic father, Rosenfeld repeatedly used this analogy: just think of the archaic emotions he has had to endure; psychosis smells bad, it is suffocating; if you think of this, you will find yourself in a better position to tolerate the emotions with which he tries to overwhelm you (Rosenfeld, Rome Seminars, 1975–1985). As is known, there are psychic elements that are essentially primitive, intractable, or simply so dangerous that they are not easily usable for mental integration. Thus, in all of our interactions, we either have to restrict within our limitations whatever it is that we have to confront, or else we have to expand our inner capacities for containment and processing. As Ferro iterates, either we have to diminish the contents or else upgrade the processing container (Ferro, Rome Seminar, 2007). This is a challenge for both analytic technique and for psychic growth.

Paradoxically, we could say that most people, including therapists, face choices comparable to those of the mentally ill person. Grotstein tries to summarise this predicament in a hypothetical collective statement, as if an emissary of the more severely suffering people were saying, "The truth of the matter is that I cannot face truth because I know the truth all too well, having not been sufficiently shielded from it, and I know the limitations of my inner resources (my alpha function) to deal with it—and this is the truth" (Grotstein, 2007, p. 296).

Suffering has an enhancing function, even though we commonly hope that our beloved children should not have to suffer. Inner travail sustains the evolution of consciousness and the burning up of our surpassed ego. When we accept suffering, however, there is an acceleration of the process that is induced by the fact that we suffer consciously. In the process of conscious suffering, there is already a measure of transformation. The fire of suffering could become the light of consciousness. The ego simply says that we should not have to suffer. But it is a distortion of the truth, which is often paradoxical. The truth is that we need to say yes to suffering before we can transcend it. We hardly ever understand what a gift the painful moments are. Without them, it would be difficult to discover any inner spark, any ember of resilience. Our future is in jeopardy at any moment and it frequently depends on our less or more creative use of pain, our willingness to travel through it. Dante's medieval poem written in common language is essentially about this challenging journey.

Construction and deconstruction

We commonly believe that the sooner our young ones develop mature ego functions, the better it is for their psychic lives. My thesis here is a corollary to this belief. If we invoke some hypothetical point in our life cycle, a time of accomplished self-formation, the process of self-de-creation should immediately be initiated, and not delayed. Perhaps a delay in self-de-creation might be as serious as a problem of delay in the development of our egos. Our well-formed egos might be regarded as the admirable result of our struggle for survival and success; yet, once a managerial ego has been accomplished, this might go on functioning indefinitely by enforcing the established policies even to the point where they can be detrimental to the continuation of our creativity—from the stage of functional maturity to the end of life. But then, the question is whether or not it is possible to let go of a functional ego, or parts of it; that could feel like psychically dying, and, thus, much too painful. In fact, once the ego solidifies into an identity, it does not want to let go, for it would feel like an inner collapse. In fact, we all find innumerable ways to deny, postpone, or overcome this "death business". Similarly, as ego development is so strenuously won, it is quite natural for us to oppose its own deconstruction. We could, perhaps, invoke in this connection one of Jung's many inspiring suggestions: "From the middle of life onward, only remains vitally alive he who is ready to *die with life*" (Jung, 1934, p. 407, my emphasis).

There are individuals who excel and who reach a stellar position in any micro- or macro-community. It is possible that these subjects would greatly benefit from a process of self-de-creation, however partial and gradual: it would be an alternative to remaining constrained in their interlocking personal and professional structures of success. At the extreme, they could turn into caricatures of themselves. People are often so identified with the thoughts that make up their world view that their thinking solidifies into mental positions infused with a sense of self. Once this has happened, we strenuously defend our convictions—our vaunted "identity". We feel and act as if we were defending our entire personality and psychic life. The ego seeks to reify, to hold, to fix, in the effort to manage anxiety, even though our whole psyche tends to surpass these convictions. The more we invest in a static concept of ourselves and of our lives, the more likely it is that we will suffer boredom. Our psyche will not be contained or fixed; it is dynamic and not static, equally capable of construction and deconstruction. In Hollis's view, it is daring, and even loving, to acknowledge that what is repeatedly paralysed in our relationships resides in ourselves (Hollis, 2003). Such recognition is almost heroic, because it requires enormous strength to take on the (moral) burden of one's shadow and destiny instead of placing it upon others. It is somehow "loving" because it frees others from the burden of carrying our own historic, existential agenda.

Reflecting on psychotherapeutic failures, Gold highlights how most papers convey an initial sense of certainty about the assessment of cases, including the patients' personal needs (Gold, 1995, quoted in Downing, 2000, p. 248). This confidence is particularly striking in comparison to the therapist's later realisation that something significant has been missed. Gold then accounts for this discrepancy by suggesting that this is essentially the discovery of our limitations: the recognition that our favoured theories and techniques simply do not apply well to a given situation. But, at times, this is too painful for us to accept. This attitude might even prompt denials and a flight into a kind of overly optimistic confidence. Yet, paradoxically, the convictions of the therapist are inseparable from the practice of psychotherapy. Within the flux of any professional life, there are drastic episodes of revision, of "revolution", or, according to mathematical models, of "catastrophe" if we can accept them. According to Steiner, these catastrophes "also manifest energies of acceleration, of metamorphoses so vehement, so far-reaching as to make . . . our explanatory theories . . . at best conjectural" (Steiner, 2002, p. 217). The paradox can be stated thus: we can only work if we are convinced, but also we cannot work if we do not allow for the devolution of convictions. And while some firm beliefs that we are attached to may not strike us as particularly important in the abstract, or in prospect, they loom large, like enormous personal involvements, when we have to make decisions and risk a loss. Why should we lose something? What nonsense! As is well known, losses hurt more than gains will gratify. This can be an immobilising logic that conspires with our uncreative way of coping with pain. Davies again: "Despite the enormous cultural pressures coercing us to ascend, there are those who descend nonetheless" (Davies, 2012, p. 124). Their descent into creative suffering can potentially generate ways of being that customary rules of life hold safely in check. Just as there are attitudes that are encouraged, there are also attitudes that are almost forbidden. These emotional propensities simply have no place in successful lives, as they are inconsistent with the need to ensure optimum performance and stability. Of course, there are emotional attitudes that are encouraged on stage, or at congresses, and "descending" emotions that are not. But this is not what we object to. What is barely visible *and* pervasive, perfectly plausible *and* damaging, is a shared, invisible obsession for unstoppably progressing in our ventures at all costs: ascend we must, the obsession intimates.

The constructive assumptions sustaining liberal optimism cannot claim immunity from challenge (Haybron, 2010, p. 250). These assumptions might, in fact, be unwarranted and we cannot take them for granted. Perhaps rationalistic, optimistic views will turn out to be not only wrong but seriously damaging. We might, in some hypothetic fullness of time, conclude that our civilisation is rooted in a mistaken view of human nature and of what we need to flourish, as if we established a habitat unsuitable to human beings. We should want, rather, to rethink how it makes sense for creatures like us to live. This inertial compulsion to ascend dominates us in an inconspicuous way, through the force of repetition. If you repeat something enough times, it becomes a psychic habit with a life of its own—it is easier to do it than not to do it. Roughly, this is Freud's well-known repetition compulsion, and even if we make it conscious, it does not subside. We like to think we react to the world as it is, when, in fact, we react to a world that primarily exists in our own minds. With all of our psychic energy focused on worrying about success, creative work is a luxury we cannot afford; in fact, there is always some dire problem demanding our attention. Every problem seems to be of life-and-death importance, but no one can see that but you. At the extreme, you cannot trust anyone to help you with your problems because no one can take them as seriously as you do.

But then, the question of the second half of life is quite different: what, now, does the soul ask of me? The person who clings to the values and idols of the first half of life may remain locked into a regressive and self-alienating pattern in which one colludes in the violation of one's more profound summons. No one has spoken more eloquently than Jung on the psychology of the second half of life. Our society prepares us for the first half by calling us to an identification with roles, but gives almost no direction for the second half: "We have no schools for forty-year-olds . . . Whoever carries over into the afternoon, the law of morning . . . must pay for it with damage to his soul" (Jung, 1934, p. 399). There is, indeed, an overemphasis on the maintenance of our egos and not enough on our capacities for deconstruction. Not surprisingly, the most obnoxious interlocutors for us in recovering our creative suffering are people whose creativity is still blocked and who adhere to surpassed structures. Our recovery almost threatens them. Even though they may be jealous of our recovery, they are still getting a payoff from remaining blocked; they can still "enjoy" sympathy and self-pity. We should not expect our blocked partners to applaud our awakening and deconstructive recovery.

Repetition compulsion revisited

The recent history of women, or of any group with insufficient negotiation power, seems to suggest that, yes, one must adapt and endure any difficulty so that one can use the adaptation *and* employ it for attaining a greater co-existential force. The story goes like this: do not be crushed by "panzers", just adapt and survive so that you can better fight for yourself. This would be the force of maturational innovations—as contrasted with oppressive traditions. We shall invoke here Jung's *Symbols of Transformation* to explore our propensity for repetition: perhaps a repetition compulsion that constantly opposes our healthier forward motions. In Jung's view, the libido that does not propel us forward but "regresses to the parents produces symptoms and situations that can only be regarded as incestuous. This is the source of all those incestuous relationships with which mythology swarms" (Jung, 1912, p. 174). But it is not only that incestuous propensities inspire our mythologies, they especially oppose our forward moving efforts—psychic development, ultimately. The inclination to repeat seems to have a gravitational power that is difficult to oppose. Yet, for good or for ill, we constantly use our tendency to repeat. The reason why this incestuous regression is so easy "seems to lie in the specific inertia of the libido, which will relinquish no object of the past, but would like to hold it fast forever . . . This inertia, as Larochefoucauld says, is also a passion" (Jung, 1912, p.174), a passion that I would call an unfortunate form of passivity. But then, a generalised phobia of inner pain seems ubiquitously to prevail *and* conspire with this inclination and all of this is vulnerable to obscurity. Paradoxically, pain does not really cause us any damage in comparison to passivity, perversion, and immobility. The pseudo-alternative to incestuous attitudes is to attach our libido to parental figures, institutions, and functions. We do marry, of course, outside of the family, but we may remain psychically linked to archaic parental representatives. Here again, as usual, it is a question of balancing proportions. When our moving forward is unduly impeded, we then gravitate towards regressive attachments.

All clusters of power show strong resistance to new behaviour that is somehow inconsistent with entrenched convictions. When we do resist anti-maturational powers but do not carefully conceal our behaviour, we will eventually be pathologised, demonised, or openly rejected. What we absolutely need is some (minimal) inner locus for the creative management of our own psychic pain. What do we mean by "management"? We are speaking of the effort of doing something with inner pain that may enhance one's psychic life. Doing something is here contrasted with just doing nothing—the worst of all options. While Larochefoucauld thinks of inertia as a sort of passion, he also insists that

> Of all the passions we are exposed to, none is more concealed from our knowledge than Idleness. It is the most violent, and the most mischievous of any, and yet at the same time we are never sensible of

its Violence, and the damage we sustain by it is very seldom seen. (Jung, 1912, p. 174)

Quite so.
Jung also presents the converging view that

If we consider its Power carefully it will be found upon all Occasions, to reign over all our Sentiments, our Interests and our Pleasures . . . The Ease and Quiet of Sloth is a secret Charm upon the Soul, to suspend its most secret Pursuits, and take its most peremptory Resolutions. (Jung, 1912, p. 174)

This dangerous passion is what lies hidden beneath the hazardous mask of incest, acquiescence, and repetition. In Jung's words, "For out of the miasmas arising from the stagnant pools of libido are born the baneful phantasmagorias which so vein reality that all adaptation becomes impossible" (Jung, 1912, p. 175). As a "sin", sloth seems truly "deadly"—in fact, deadening. But then, Nirmala was not in the least lazy, and certainly not slothful or incestuous.

If we consider the Scriptures as indicating remedies for the psychopathology of the west, of course there is no question as to why sloth is regarded as a "deadly sin". It precisely deadens our psyche. No forward motion is possible under the auspices of its secret spell. But then, in the recent history of women (or of any group that is opportunely excluded from power), there seems to be an avoidance of any form of its spell, or mystique. It is suggested that, yes, we should adapt and endure just about everything, *but* in order to make a creative use of the suffering that adaptation requires. A pragmatic voice seems to counsel, "Do not be crushed by superpowers, just try to adapt so that you can survive and thus/then fight for yourself, *and* transform *for* yourself the psychic pain that you manage to endure". Our psychic pain can be induced whenever the varying conditions to which we struggle to submit (for the sake of adaptation) are not rewarding, but, in fact, merely punishing. In this sense, inner suffering is not to be understood as a sign of mental disorder, but, rather, as an indication that we are very much alive, that we resent a condition which does not allow any forward movement. In Nirmala's case, her adaptation should have been submission to the injunction not to exist. She moved forward, none the less, because she was not deadened by sloth. She managed always to do something, with whatever means.

An oscillating balance was sought between the improvement of conditions and the relative intensity of pain. Yet, even in a sequence of fluctuations, the decisive factor for psychic growth is primarily dependent on our capacity to endure and use our inner labours, avoid default, and move forward.

Sit finis operis, non finis quaerendi.

REFERENCES

A'Kempis, T. (1952). *Imitation of Christ*, L. Sherley-Price (Trans.). London: Penguin.
Alighieri, D. (1958). *The Inferno*, J. A. Carlyle (Trans.). London: J. M. Dent.
Aristotle (1985). *The Complete Works of Aristotle Vol. II*, revised Oxford translation, J. Barnes (Ed.). Princeton, NJ: Princeton University Press.
Baggini, J. (2010). *Complaint. From Minor Moans to Principled Protests*. London: Profile Books.
Benjamin, J. (1990). *The Bonds of Love: Psychoanalysis, Feminism and the Problem of Domination*. London: Virago.
Bion, W. R. (1962). A theory of thinking. *International Journal of Psychoanalysis*, 43: 306–310.
Bion, W. R. (1970). *Attention and Interpretation. A Scientific Approach to Insight in Psycho-Analysis and Groups*. London: Tavistock.
Bion, W. R. (2005). *The Tavistock Seminars*, F. Bion (Ed.). London: Karnac.
Brontë, A. (1994). Preface. *The Tenant of Wildfell Hall* (2nd edn). London: Penguin.
Cancrini, T. (2002). *Un tempo per il dolore: Eros, dolore e colpa*. Turin: Bollati Boringhieri.
Caper, R. (1999). *A Mind of One's Own: A Kleinian View of Self and Object*. London: Routledge.

Chang, J. (1991). *Wild Swans: Three Daughters of China*. London: HarperCollins.
Corradi, S., & Madia, I. (2003). *Un percorso di auto-educazione: materiali per una bio-bibliografia di Mario Verdone*. Rome: Aracne Editrice.
Corradi Fiumara, G. (1990). *The Other Side of Language: A Philosophy of Listening*. London: Routledge.
Corradi Fiumara, G. (1992). *The Symbolic Function: Psychoanalysis and the Philosophy of Language*. Oxford: Blackwell.
Corradi Fiumara, G. (1995). *The Metaphoric Process: Connections Between Language and Life*. London: Routledge.
Corradi Fiumara, G. (2009). *Spontaneity: A Psychoanalytic Inquiry*. London: Routledge.
Corradi Fiumara, G. (2013). *Psychoanalysis and Creativity in Everyday Life: Ordinary Genius*. London: Routledge.
Cyrulnik, B. (2003). *The Whispering of Ghosts. Trauma and Resilience*. New York: Other Press.
Davies, J. (2012). *The Importance of Suffering: The Value and Meaning of Emotional Discontent*. London: Routledge.
De Monticelli, R. (2003). *L'ordine del cuore: Etica e teoria del sentire*. Milan: Garzanti.
Dobbs, D. (2011). Beautiful brains. *National Geographic, 220*: 4.
Dobelli, R. (2013). *The Art of Thinking Clearly*, N. Griffin (Trans.). London: Sceptre/Hodder & Stoughton.
Downing, J. N. (2000). *Between Conviction and Uncertainty. Philosophical Guidelines for the Practicing Psychotherapist*. Albany, NY: State University of New York Press.
Eigen, M. (2001). *Damaged Bonds*. London: Karnac.
Ferro, A. (2011). *Avoiding Emotions, Living Emotions*, J. Harvey (Trans.). London: Routledge.
Frankl, V. E. (2007). *Man's Search for Meaning. Part One*, I. Lasch (Trans.). London: Rider.
Freud, S. (1916d). Some character types met with in psychoanalytic work. *S. E., 14*: 309–336.
Freud, S. (1920g). *Beyond the Pleasure Principle. S. E., 18*: 7–64. London: Hogarth.
Freud, S. (1926d). *Inhibitions, Symptoms and Anxiety. S. E., 20*: 77–174. London: Hogarth.
Freud, S. (1927c). *The Future of an Illusion. S. E., 21*: 3–56. London: Hogarth.
Freud, S. (1928b). Dostoevsky and parricide. *S. E., 21*: 175–196. London: Hogarth.

Freud, S. (1930a). *Civilization and its Discontents. S. E., 21*: 59–145. London: Hogarth.

Fromm, E. (1995). *To Have Or To Be?* New York: Abacus.

Gold, J. R. (1995). Knowing and not knowing: commentary on the roots of psychotherapeutic failure. *Journal of Psychotherapy Integration, 5*: 167–170.

Grotstein, J. S. (2007). *A Beam of Intense Darkness: Wilfred Bion's Legacy to Psychoanalysis*. London: Karnac.

Grotstein, J. S. (2009). *". . . But At The Same Time And On Another Level . . .": Clinical Applications in the Kleinian/Bionian Mode* (Volume Two). London: Karnac.

Haraway, D. (1996). *Modest Witness@Second Millenium. Female Man Meets Oncomouse TM: Feminism and Technoscience*. London: Routledge.

Haybron, D. M. (2010). *The Pursuit of Unhappiness: The Elusive Psychology of Well-Being*. Oxford: Oxford University Press.

Hegel, G. W. F. (1977). *The Phenomenology of the Spirit*, A. V. Miller (Trans.). Oxford: Oxford University Press.

Hesse, H. (1990). *The Glass Bead Game: Magister Ludi*, R. & C. Winston (Trans.). New York: Picador.

Hesse, H. (1997). *La nevrosi si può vincere*, O. Bernardi (Trans.). Milan: Mondadori.

Hollis, J. (2003). *On this Journey We Call Our Life. Living the Questions*. Toronto: Inner City Books.

Hood, B. (2011). *The Self Illusion: Who Do You Think You Are?* London: Constable.

Jung, C. G. (1912). *Symbols of Transformation*. London: Routledge & Kegan Paul.

Jung, C. G. (1934). *The Structure and Dynamics of the Psyche*. London: Routledge & Kegan Paul.

Jung, C. G. (1936). *Civilization in Transition*. London: Routledge & Kegan Paul.

Jung, C. G. (1951). *Aion: Researches into the Phenomenology of the Self*. London: Routledge & Kegan Paul.

Jung, C. G. (1955). *Mysterium Coniunctionis: An Inquiry into the Separation and Synthesis of Opposites in Alchemy*. London: Routledge and Kegan Paul.

Kahneman, D. (2011). *Thinking, Fast and Slow*. London: Penguin.

Kierkegaard, S. (1962). *Works of Love*, H. & E. Hong (Trans.). New York: Harperperennial.

Kierkegaard, S. (1996). *Papers and Journals: A Selection*. London: Penguin.

Klein, M. (1964). *Contributions to Psycho-Analysis 1921–1945*. New York: McGraw-Hill.

Laplanche, J., & Pontalis, J.-B. (1973). *The Language of Psychoanalysis*, D. Nicholson-Smith (Trans.). London: Hogarth Press.

Leary, D. E. (Ed.) (1990). *Metaphors in the History of Psychology*. Cambridge: Cambridge University Press.

Lewis, C. S. (2012). *The Problem of Pain*. London: HarperCollins..

Maslow, A. H. (1968). *Toward a Psychology of Being* (2nd edn). New York: Van Norstrand Reinhold.

McDougall, J. (1990). *Plaidoyer pour une certaine anormalité*. Paris: Editions Gallimard.

Meltzer, D. W. (1992). *The Claustrum: An Investigation of Claustrophobic Phenomena*. Strathtay, Perthshire: Clunie Press.

Meng, H., & Freud, E. L. (Eds.) (1963). *Psycho-Analysis and Faith: The Letters of Sigmund Freud and Oskar Pfister*, E. Mosbacher (Trans.). London: The Hogarth Press and the Institute of Psycho-Analysis.

Midgley, M. (1984). *Wickedness: A Philosophical Essay*. London: Routledge.

Nietzsche, F. (1979). *Philosophy and Truth: Selection from Nietzsche's Notebooks of the Early 1870s*. Atlantic, NJ: Humanities Press.

Oliver, K. (2004). *The Colonization of Psychic Space: A Psychoanalytic Social Theory of Oppression*. Minneapolis, MN: University of Minnesota Press.

Padoa-Schioppa, T. (2006). *Europa una pazienza attiva. Malinconia e riscatto del Vecchio Continente*. Milan: Rizzoli.

Pascal, B. (1995). *Human Happiness*, A. J. Krailsheimer (Trans.). London: Penguin.

Phillips, A. (1988). *Winnicott*. London: Fontana.

Phillips, A. (2002). *Houdini's Box: On the Arts of Escape*. London: Faber and Faber.

Phillips, A. (2004). *Going Sane*. London: Penguin.

Phillips, A., & Taylor, B. (2009). *On Kindness*. London: Penguin.

Sandel, M. (2012). *What Money Can't Buy: The Moral Limits of Markets*. London: Penguin.

Segal, H. (1979). *Klein*. London: Fontana Modern Masters.

Sen, A. (2009). *The Idea of Justice*. Cambridge, MA: Harvard University Press.

Solzhenitsyn, A. (1974). *The Gulag Archipelago*, T. P. Whitney (Trans.). Paris: Editions du Seuil.

Spar, D. (2013). Fear of failing. *Barnard Alumnae Magazine*, 1: 3–7.

Steiner, G. (2002). *Grammars of Creation*. London: Faber and Faber.

Stern, D. N. (2004). *The Present Moment: In Psychotherapy and Everyday Life*. New York: W. W. Norton.

Stevenson, R. L. (2002). *The Strange Case of Dr. Jekyll and Mr. Hyde*. Florence: Giunti Editore.
Storr, A. (1997). *Solitude*. London: HarperCollins.
Symington, N. (2001). *The Spirit of Sanity*. London: Karnac.
Symington, N. (2002). *A Pattern of Madness*. London: Karnac.
Symington, N. (2004). *The Blind Man Sees: Freud's Awakening and Other Essays*. London: Karnac.
Thiele Rolando, R. (1982). *Dolore. Che cosa significa? Perché lo rifiutiamo? Come viverlo?* Milan: Rizzoli.
Winnicott, D. W. (1958). *Collected Papers: Through Paediatrics to Psycho-Analysis*. London: Tavistock.
Winnicott, D. W. (1970). Cure. In: *Home Is Where We Start From: Essays by a Psychoanalyst*. London: Pelican.
Winnicott, D. W. (1971). *Playing and Reality*. London: Tavistock.
Wittgenstein, L. (1981). *Tractatus Logico-Philosophicus*. P. F. Pears & B. McGuinness (Trans.). London: Routledge and Kegan Paul.
Wright, K. (2009). *Mirroring and Attunement: Self-Realization in Psychoanalysis and Art*. London: Routledge.
Yalom, I. D. (2011). *The Gift of Therapy*. London: Piatkus.

INDEX

abuse, 16, 50, 64, 67, 106, 109–110
affect(ive), 63, 67, 133
   acceptance, 146
   communications, 132
   distress, xii
   focus, 93
   growth, 126
   hunger, 55
   inner, 146
   integration of, 93, 145
   investment, 131
   maturity, 56
   negative, 144
   pain, 56, 93
   primitive, 144
   problems, xxiv
   space, xi
   troublesome, 56
   unbearable, 154
aggression, 9, 11, 24, 37, 66, 129, 131–132 *see also*: emotion(al)
   behaviour, 131

A'Kempis, T., 105
Alighieri, D., 153
anaesthesia, xiv, xix, xxii, xxiv–xxv, xxvii, 4, 12, 17, 19–22, 24–26, 28–32, 34, 51–52, 55–56, 68, 71, 75, 85, 87–88, 92, 104, 143, 149
   chemical, xxv
   consumption of, xxvii
   contemporary, 21
   corrective, 22
   effective, 30, 91
   emotional, 34
   function, 31
   ideology, xxvii, 36
   immediate, 25
   perfect, 22
   powerful, 85, 107
   psychic, 17, 24, 28, 88
   regime, 29
   remedial, 23, 108
   strategy, xxvii

stupefying, 10
symptomatic, 41
temporary, 22
anxiety, xiii–xiv, xxiii–xxiv, 12, 20, 23,
  31, 71, 85, 90, 114–115, 124,
  133–134, 157
Aristotle, 118
attachment, 18, 46, 58, 96, 100,
  102–103, 125, 132–133, 135, 155,
  158, 160

Baggini, J., 9, 50, 94, 108
behaviour, xxvii, 56, 131, 148, 160
  see also: aggression
  abusive, 16
  bad, 97
  dissolute, 75
  hostile, 125
  intoxicating, 151
  irresponsible, 20
  maddening, 149
  modification of, xxii
  schizo–paranoid, 37
Benjamin, J., 115
Bion, W. R., xiv, xxviii, 7, 22, 24–26,
  104–105, 113–114, 119, 125–127,
  140
Brontë, A., 67, 73

Cancrini, T., 128–130
Caper, R., 105
case studies
  Nirmala, xv, 99–104, 113–114, 119,
    121, 161
  Percival, xv, 61–66, 125
  Sara, xv, 15–20, 129–130
Chang, J., 9, 35–36
conscious(ness), xxii, 10, 29, 58, 69–70,
  72, 82, 88–89, 112, 127, 132,
  151, 155–156, 158 *see also*:
  unconscious(ness)
  absence of, 69
  beneficial, xxii
  level, xiii

mind, 69
personality, 70
self-, 74, 79–82
suffering, 156
Corradi, S., 142
Corradi Fiumara, G., xiii, 2, 48, 88,
  108, 117, 122–123, 125
Cyrulnik, B., 132

Davies, J., xvi, xviii, xx–xxv, 4, 6,
  10, 12, 23–24, 26, 28–30, 34,
  44–45, 52, 68, 85, 104–105,
  107, 131–132, 141–142, 154–155,
  158
De Monticelli, R., 146
death, 81, 153–154, 156
  fear of, 27, 56
  instinct, 37–38
  life-and-, 81, 159
  pain of, 88
  psychic(ally), 71
depressive, 141
  outlook, 112
  pain, 22
  position, 22–23, 55, 111–113
  states, 22
desire, xxvi, 8, 21, 34–35, 42, 53–55,
  91, 93–94, 96, 105, 111, 124, 132,
  139 *see also*: paranoid
  celebrated, 7
  natural, 34
  unquestionable, xvii
destiny, 25, 40–42, 46–51, 53, 144,
  157
  personal, 40, 45–47, 49–51
  pseudo-, 46
  unique, 50
development(al), xx, 8, 22, 40, 47, 80,
  87, 103, 106–107, 114, 118, 120,
  124–125, 128, 132, 141, 143–144,
  150, 154, 156
  child, 113
  ego, 156
  human, 23

mental, 119
neurological, 149
normal, 113
personal, 55
psychic(ally), 82, 147, 160
Dobbs, D., 148–150
Dobelli, R., 96–97, 108, 111
Downing, J. N., xvi, 117, 157

ego, 30, 37, 50, 68, 72, 108, 113,
       156–157, 159 *see also*:
       development(al)
   fragile, 37
   functions, 156
   limited, 45
   managerial, 156
   primitive, 37
   smart, 108
   super, 37
Eigen, M., 147
emancipation, xvii, 4, 31, 38, 85,
       153
   inner, 139, 153
   social, 42
emotion(al), 10, 22, 36, 70, 94,
       118–119, 123, 128–129, 145,
       154–155 *see also*: suffering
   aggression, 154
   archaic, 16, 129, 146, 151, 155
   avoidance of, 10, 123, 154
   descending, 158
   difficult, 11–12, 141, 145
   dire, 134
   experience, 93, 112
   explosion of, 133
   force, 129
   impact, 11
   indigestible, 10
   intensity, 8
   intolerable, 153
   intractable, 155
   itinerary, 8
   living, 52, 123
   miniaturisation of, 10

misery, 3
nutrients, 147
overwhelming, 144, 154
pain, xiii, 11
primitive, 17
propensities, 158
proto-, 11–12, 107, 128–131, 134,
       145, 155
reweaving, 134
threatening, 108, 111
torment, xxv
unbearable, 134
uncontainability of, 131
urgency, 131

Ferro, A., xx–xxi, 10–11, 51–52, 71,
       73, 106–107, 114, 118–119,
       123–124, 128–134, 141, 145,
       154–155
Frankl, V. E., 36, 42
Freud, E. L., 57
Freud, S., xiii, xxiii, 21–24, 46, 48,
       57, 78–79, 83, 86, 89–90,
       109–110, 114–115, 122, 129,
       138, 158
Fromm, E., xvi–xviii, 44

Gold, J. R., 157
Grotstein, J. S., xxvii–xxviii, 24, 37,
       111–112, 133, 155
guilt, 16, 23, 63, 66, 92, 109, 114
       see also: unconscious(ness)
   absurd, 92
   communal, 92
   corporate, 92
   old-fashioned, 92
   personal, 92
   projected, 92
   sense of, 92

Haraway, D., 56
Haybron, D. M., xii, xvi, 23–24,
       50–52, 158
Hegel, G. W. F., xv, 5, 78–83, 89

Hesse, H., 21, 84, 87, 89
Hollis, J., xix, 6, 10, 48, 67, 106, 119, 140, 155, 157
Hood, B., 47–48, 118

James, W., 68, 107, 132
Jung, C. G., xxii, 6, 22, 48, 67–70, 72–74, 86, 156, 159–161
justice, 42, 45, 47
   emancipatory, 49, 54–55
   in-, 32, 40, 42–44, 51, 139
      material, 43
      psychic, 44
      remedial, 43
      systemic, 41
      tangible, 53
      total, 50
   perfect, 40
   psychic, 39–42, 47
   sense of, 39
   social, xvii, 44, 55
   ultimate, 42

Kahneman, D., xxvi–xxvii, 96–97, 111
Kierkegaard, S., xxii, 2, 6, 46, 48, 112
Klein, M., xiv, 22–23, 80, 86, 112–113

Laplanche, J., 120
Leary, D. E., 122
Lewis, C. S., xv, xx, 20–21, 29, 33, 92, 127

Madia, I., 142
Maslow, A. H., 6
McDougall, J., 109, 147
Meltzer, D. W., xxxviii
Meng, H., 57
Midgley, M., 72, 75
mode
   being, xviii–xix, 44–45
   everyday, xi
   having, xvii–xviii, 45

   of existence, xviii
   of knowing, 117
mother, 16, 18, 22, 47, 64–65, 78–79, 81, 88–89, 101, 103, 106–107, 130, 133
   dead, 130
   figure, 106
   fragile, 19
   heroic, 43
   hypothetic, 132
   good, 53
   grand, 9
   poor, 16, 101
   psychotic, 129–130
   suicidal, 43
mourning, xiii, 9, 19, 88, 105

Nietzsche, F., 121

object(ive), xiii, 29, 34, 36–37, 41, 45, 48, 83–84, 103, 105, 108, 123, 133, 143, 147, 158, 160
   desirable, 37
   detached, 46
   good, 37–38
   lost, 105
   loved, 105
   psychoanalytic, 83
   reality, 121
   relations, 77
   transitional, 140
   useful, 37
   utterances, 123
Oedipus, 55, 80, 82–83, 85, 121, 124
   complex, 23
Oliver, K., 151

Padoa-Schioppa, T., 10
paranoid, xvii, 41, 45, 55
   conviction, xviii
   delusions, 144
   desire, xvii
   disorders, 71
   outlook, xviii–xix

Pascal, B., 27, 33, 42, 49–50, 135
Phillips, A., xxii–xxiii, xxv, 11, 22–23, 29, 53–54, 77–78, 83, 86, 106–107, 112, 141, 147
Pontalis, J.-B., 120
projection, 67, 69–72, 92, 112, 132, 134
 idealising, 25
 reactive, 69
projective, xvii
 furores, 73
 identification, xxvii, 70–71, 130
 inclinations, 72
 strategies, 69
 tricks, 112
psychic(ally) *see also*: death, development(al)
 actions, xviii, xxi, 5, 8, 69, 80, 83, 106, 108, 112–113, 139
 activity, 7
 adversity, 55
 agency, 2
 agenda, 74
 anaesthesia, 17, 24, 28, 88
 atmosphere, 57, 155
 attitude, 67
 burden, 74
 capacity, 114
 colonisation, 55
 condition, 57, 94, 141
 confidence, 132
 consuming, 21
 contingency, 117
 creativity, xix
 currents, 147
 deadening, 124
 difficulties, 56
 dimensions, 44, 58
 discontent, 35, 40
 distress, xi, 23, 46, 97
 domain, 55–56, 58, 147
 drama, 50
 dynamics, 56
 earthquakes, 150
 effort, 127

elements, 128, 155
energy, 43, 158–159
enslavement, 53
entropy, 55
equity, 40, 42
evolution, 7
experience, 50
famine, 51
forces, 41–42, 69, 138
foreclusion, 126
form, 113, 115
fulfilment, 50
gaze, 53
growth, xxvii, 3, 45, 48, 119, 131, 155, 162
habit, 158
harmony, 56
hatred, 81
health, 42, 135
hunger, 54
inequalities, 47
injustice, 44
instrument, 119
interaction, 80
intimacy, 58
intra-, xxvii, 124
intrusion, 70
justice, 39–40, 42, 47
labour, 22
level, 44, 54, 133, 148–149
life, xii, xix, 21, 31, 44, 80, 124–125, 130, 137, 143–144, 151, 156–157, 160
locus, 96
luxury, 7
metabolism, 144
moves, 89
offence, 54
oppression, 55
pain, xiii, xv–xvi, xix, xxi, xxiv, 1, 3, 21, 23–24, 36, 41, 45, 48, 52, 58, 66, 69–70, 72–74, 84–85, 88–89, 91, 128–129, 139, 142, 153, 160–161

paradoxes, 112
paralysis, 74
passivity, 46
poor, 39–40, 42, 44
position, 81
poverty, 40
problems, xv, 51
quality, 140
reactions, 106
reality, xxviii, 22, 51, 55, 117
relief, 131
resources, 39
revolver, 11–12
rich, 40, 90
side-effects, 111
sloth, 9
space, xxvii, 134, 151
states, 23, 64
strangulation, 132
strength, 21
stupor, 8
suffering, xi, 2, 11, 26, 34, 54, 56, 119, 123, 149
survival, 2, 55
survivors, 109
symptoms, 29
threats, 111
tissue, 128–129
touch, 132
transformations, xviii
tribulation, 1, 69
truth, 135
vicissitudes, xv, 56–57, 83, 147

repression, xiv, 67, 154

Sandel, M., 23–24, 27
schizoid
  attitudes, 42
  –paranoid *see also*: behaviour
    attitudes, 111, 141
    reactions, 4
    ventures, 22
Segal, H., 22

self, 2, 17, 21, 26, 31, 42, 53–54, 64, 66–69, 71, 74–78, 86, 91–93, 120
  see also: conscious(ness)
-accusation, 103
-actualizing, 6
-adherence, 127
-alienating, 159
certainty, 79
constricted, 68
-created, 142
-cure, 29
-damaging, 75–76
-deadening, xiv, 83
-deception, 35
-deconstructing, xxvi
-de-creation, 156–157
deeper, 50, 91
-defeating, xvii, 139
-definition, 80
-destructive, 67, 84
-directed, 23
-discovery, 90
-education, 142
entire, 12
-esteem, 18, 23, 27, 43, 57, 91
-expression, xxi
false, 67, 125
-formation, xxvi, 22, 120, 156
-healing, 123
higher, 68
ideal, 102
individual, 47
innermost, 19
-interest, 86, 148
-knowledge, 73
-loathing, 18
-pity, 159
psychic, 58
-realization, 90
receptive, 73
-referential, 119
secluded, 66
second, 66
sense of, 6, 53, 157

shadowy, 22, 69
successful, 19
-treatment, 144
-trust, 142
-willed, 53
Sen, A., 40, 43–46, 55, 102
sexual(ly)
  abusive, 16
  contact, 146
  domain, 78
  encounter, 95
  harassing, 16
  interpretations, 146
  life, 53, 78
  relations, 78
sexuality, 54, 58–59, 78
Solzhenitsyn, A., 36, 42
Spar, D., 58–59
splitting, 5, 22, 52, 64, 75–76, 82
Steiner, G., 157–158
Stern, D. N., 130
Stevenson, R. L., 75–76
Storr, A., 48, 78, 86–87, 90, 93
suffering (*passim*) *see also*:
    conscious(ness)
  absence of, xxv
  authentic, 19
  creative, xxiv, xxvi, 1–5, 7, 12, 24,
    27, 29, 41, 45, 85, 104, 110–111,
    133, 138, 158–159
  elimination of, 35
  emotional, 23, 52
  existential, xiii
  fruitful, 3
  human, xiii–xiv, xix, xxii, xxv–xxvi,
    9, 41, 72, 90, 93, 124
  inherent, 84
  inner, xxv, 4, 30, 84, 161
  mental, xv

productive, 4, 10, 29
psychic, xi, 2, 11, 26, 34, 54, 56, 119,
  123, 149
unavoidable, xvi
uncreative, xiii, xxiv, xxvii, 2, 6–7,
  12, 85
unproductive, xxv, 4, 10, 29–30
symbol(-ism), xii, 84, 106, 120, 122,
  125, 134
Symington, N., xx, 32, 70, 76, 141

Taylor, B., 53–54, 86
Thiele Rolando, R., 3, 137
transference, xxviii, 124, 128–129
  see also: unconscious(ness)
  –countertransference, 86, 134
  engaging, 127
  psychotic, 131

unconscious(ness), xiii, 24, 69, 76,
  107, 109, 112 *see also*
  conscious(ness)
  guilt, 92
  hatred, 105
  refusal, 31
  thoughts, 129
  transference, 48

violence, xviii, 54, 64, 76, 124, 131,
  144, 160–161

Winnicott, D. W., xxi–xxiii, xxv, 1–3,
  11, 22, 27, 43, 48, 74, 77–79, 81,
  83, 89, 106–108, 112, 132,
  140–141, 147
Wittgenstein, L., xii
Wright, K., 86, 113

Yalom, I. D., 25–26, 81–82, 84, 93